Los Angeles Dodgers 2020

A Baseball Companion

Edited by R.J. Anderson, Craig Goldstein and Bret Sayre

Baseball Prospectus

Craig Brown, Steven Goldman and David Pease, Consultant Editors
Robert Au, Harry Pavlidis and Amy Pircher, Statistics Editors

Copyright © 2020 by DIY Baseball, LLC.
All rights reserved

This book or any part thereof may not be reproduced or transmitted in any form or by any means, electronic or mechanical, including photocopying, recording, or by any information storage and retrieval system, without permission in writing from the publisher.

Limit of Liability/Disclaimer of Warranty: While the publisher and the author have used their best efforts in preparing this book, they make no representations or warranties with respect to the accuracy or completeness of the contents of this book and specifically disclaim any implied warranties of merchantability or fitness for a particular purpose. No warranty may be created or extended by sales representatives or written sales materials. The advice and strategies contained herein may not be suitable for your situation. You should consult with a professional where appropriate. Neither the publisher nor the author shall be liable for any loss of profit or any other commercial damages, including but not limited to special, incidental, consequential, or other damages.

Library of Congress Cataloging-in-Publication Data:
paperback
ISBN-13: 978-1-950716-04-3

Project Credits
Cover Design: Michael Byzewski at Aesthetic Apparatus
Interior Design and Production: Jeff Pease, Dave Pease
Layout: Jeff Pease, Dave Pease

Baseball icon courtesy of Uberux, from https://www.shareicon.net/author/uberux

Ballpark diagram courtesy of Lou Spirito/THIRTY81 Project, https://thirty81project.com/

Manufactured in the United States of America
10 9 8 7 6 5 4 3 2 1

Table of Contents

Statistical Introduction v

Part 1: Team Analysis

Los Angeles Dodgers: Where Are You Going, Where Have You Been? ... 3
    Craig Goldstein, Jeffrey Paternostro and Matthew Trueblood
Performance Graphs 7
2019 Team Performance 8
2020 Team Projections 9
Team Personnel 10
Dodger Stadium Stats 11
Dodgers Team Analysis 13

Part 2: Player Analysis

Dodgers Player Analysis 20
Dodgers Prospects 99

Part 3: Featured Articles

The Baseball Is Juiced (Again) 117
    Robert Arthur
The Moral Hazard of Playing It Safe 121
    Craig Goldstein

Index of Names 127

Statistical Introduction

Sports are, fundamentally, a blend of athletic endeavor and storytelling. Baseball, like any other sport, tells its stories in so many ways: in the arc of a game from the stands or a season from the box scores, in photos, or even in numbers. At Baseball Prospectus, we understand that statistics don't replace observation or any of baseball's stories, but complement everything else that makes the game so much fun.

What stats help us with is with patterns and precision, variance and value. This book can help you learn things you may not see from watching a game or hundred, whether it's the path of a career over time or the breadth of the entire MLB. We'd also never ask you to choose between our numbers and the experience of viewing a game from the cheap seats or the comfort of your home; our publication combines running the numbers with observations and wisdom from some of the brightest minds we can find. But if you *do* want to learn more about the numbers beyond what's on the backs of player jerseys, let us help explain.

Offense

We've revised our methodology for determining batting value. Long-time readers of the book will notice that we've retired True Average in favor of a new metric: Deserved Runs Created Plus (DRC+). Developed by Jonathan Judge and our stats team, this statistic measures everything a player does at the plate–reaching base, hitting for power, making outs, and moving runners over–and puts it on a scale where 100 equals league-average performance. A DRC+ of 150 is terrific, a DRC+ of 100 is average and a DRC+ of 75 means you better be an excellent defender.

DRC+ also does a better job than any of our previous metrics in taking contextual factors into account. The model adjusts for how the park affects performance, but also for things like the talent of the opposing pitcher, value of different types of batted-ball events, league, temperature and other factors. It's able to describe a player's expected offensive contribution than any other statistic we've found over the years, and also does a better job of predicting future performance as well.

There's a lot more to DRC+'s story, and you can read all about it in greater depth near the end of this book.

The other aspect of run-scoring is baserunning, which we quantify using Baserunning Runs. BRR not only records the value of stolen bases (or getting caught in the act), but also accounts for all the stuff that doesn't show up on the back of a baseball card: a runner's ability to go first to third on a single, or advance on a fly ball.

Defense

Where offensive value is *relatively* easy to identify and understand, defensive value is...not. Over the past dozen years, the sabermetric community has focused mostly on stats based on zone data: a real-live human person records the type of batted ball and estimated landing location, and models are created that give expected outs. From there, you can compare fielders' actual outs to those expected ones. Simple, right?

Unfortunately, zone data has two major issues. First, zone data is recorded by commercial data providers who keep the raw data private unless you pay for it. (All the statistics we build in this book and on our website use public data as inputs.) That hurts our ability to test assumptions or duplicate results. Second, over the years it has become apparent that there's quite a bit of "noise" in zone-based fielding analysis. Sometimes the conclusions drawn from zone data don't hold up to scrutiny, and sometimes the different data provided by different providers don't look anything alike, giving wildly different results. Sometimes the hard-working professional stringers or scorers might unknowingly inflict unconscious bias into the mix: for example good fielders will often be credited with more expected outs despite the data, and ballparks with high press boxes tend to score more line drives than ones with a lower press box.

Enter our Fielding Runs Above Average (FRAA). For most positions, FRAA is built from play-by-play data, which allows us to avoid the subjectivity found in many other fielding metrics. The idea is this: count how many fielding plays are made by a given player and compare that to expected plays for an average fielder at their position (based on pitcher ground ball tendencies and batter handedness). Then we adjust for park and base-out situations.

When it comes to catchers, our methodology is a little different thanks to the laundry list of responsibilities they're tasked with beyond just, well, catching and throwing the ball. By now you've probably heard about "framing" or the art of making umpires more likely to call balls outside the strike zone for strikes. To put this into one tidy number, we incorporate pitch tracking data (for the years it exists) and adjust for important factors like pitcher, umpire, batter and home-field advantage using a mixed-model approach. This grants us a number for how many strikes the catcher is personally adding to (or subtracting from) his pitchers' performance...which we then convert to runs added or lost using linear weights.

Framing is one of the biggest parts of determining catcher value, but we also take into account blocking balls from going past, whether a scorer deems it a passed ball or a wild pitch. We use a similar approach—one that really benefits from the pitch tracking data that tells us what ends up in the dirt and what doesn't. We also include a catcher's ability to prevent stolen bases and how well they field balls in play, and *finally* we come up with our FRAA for catchers.

Pitching

Both pitching and fielding make up the half of baseball that isn't run scoring: run prevention. Separating pitching from fielding is a tough task, and most recent pitching analysis has branched off from Voros McCracken's famous (and controversial) statement, "There is little if any difference among major-league pitchers in their ability to prevent hits on balls hit in the field of play." The research of the analytic community has validated this to some extent, and there are a host of "defense-independent" pitching measures that have been developed to try and extract the effect of the defense behind a hurler from the pitcher's work.

Our solution to this quandary is Deserved Run Average (DRA), our core pitching metric. DRA looks like earned run average (ERA), the tried-and-true pitching stat you've seen on every baseball broadcast or box score from the past century, but it's very different. To start, DRA takes an event-by-event look at what the pitchers does, and adjusts the value of that event based on different environmental factors like park, batter, catcher, umpire, base-out situation, run differential, inning, defense, home field advantage, pitcher role and temperature. That mixed model gives us a pitcher's expected contribution, similar to what we do for our DRC+ model for hitters and FRAA model for catchers. (Oh, and we also consider the pitcher's effect on basestealing and on balls getting past the catcher.)

It's important to note that DRA is set to the scale of runs allowed per nine innings (RA9) instead of ERA, which makes DRA's scale slightly higher than ERA's. The reason for this is because ERA tends to overrate three types of pitchers:

1. Pitchers who play in parks where scorers hand out more errors. Official scorers differ significantly in the frequency at which they assign errors to fielders.
2. Ground-ball pitchers, because a substantial proportion of errors occur on groundballs.
3. Pitchers who aren't very good. Better pitchers often allow fewer unearned runs than bad pitchers, because good pitchers tend to find ways to get out of jams.

Since the last time you picked up an edition of this book, we've also made a few minor changes to DRA to make it better. Recent research into "tunneling"—the act of throwing consecutive pitches that appear similar from a batter's point of view until after the swing decision point–data has given us a new contextual factor to account for in DRA: plate distance. This refers to the distance between successive pitches as they approach the plate, and while it has a smaller effect than factors like velocity or whiff rate, it still can help explain pitcher strikeout rate in our model.

New Pitching Metrics for 2020

We're including a few "new" pitching metrics in the book for the 2020 edition, though unlike last year, these numbers may be a little bit more familiar to those of you who have spent some time investigating baseball statistics.

Fastball Percentage

Our fastball percentage (FB%) statistic measures how frequently a pitcher throws a pitch classified as a "fastball," measured as a percentage of overall pitches thrown. We qualify three types of fastballs:

1. The traditional four-seam fastball;
2. The two-seam fastball or sinker;
3. "Hard cutters," which are pitches that have the movement profile of a cut fastball and are used as the pitcher's primary offering or in place of a more traditional fastball.

For example, a pitcher with a FB% of 67 throws any combination of these three pitches about two-thirds of the time.

Whiff Rate

Everybody loves a swing and a miss, and whiff rate (WHF) measures how frequently pitchers induce a swinging strike. To calculate WHF, we add up all the pitches thrown that ended with a swinging strike, then divide that number by a pitcher's total pitches thrown. Most often, high whiff rates correlate with high strikeout rates (and overall effective pitcher performance).

Called Strike Probability

Called Strike Probability (CSP) is a number that represents the likelihood that all of a pitcher's pitches will be called a strike while controlling for location, pitcher and batter handedness, umpire and count. Here's how it works: on each pitch, our model determines how many times (out of 100) that a similar pitch was called for a strike given those factors mentioned above, and when normalized for each batter's strike zone. Then we average the CSP for all pitches thrown by a pitcher in a season, and that gives us the yearly CSP percentage you see in the stats boxes.

As you might imagine, pitchers with a higher CSP are more likely to work in the zone, where pitchers with a lower CSP are likely locating their pitches outside the normal strike zone, for better or for worse.

Projections

Many of you aren't turning to this book just for a look at what a player has done, but for a look at what a player is going to do: the PECOTA projections. PECOTA, initially developed by Nate Silver (who has moved on to greater fame as a political analyst), consists of three parts:

1. Major-league equivalencies, which use minor-league statistics to project how a player will perform in the major leagues;
2. Baseline forecasts, which use weighted averages and regression to the mean to estimate a player's current true talent level; and
3. Aging curves, which uses the career paths of comparable players to estimate how a player's statistics are likely to change over time.

With all those important things covered, let's take a look at what's in the book this year.

Team Prospectus

Most of this book is composed of team chapters, with one for each of the 30 major-league franchises. On the first page of each chapter, you'll see a box that contains some of the key statistics for each team as well as a very inviting stadium diagram. (You can see an example of this for the Milwaukee Brewers on this very page!)

We start with the team name, their unadjusted 2019 win-loss record, and their divisional ranking. Beneath that are a host of other team statistics. **Pythag** presents an adjusted 2019 winning percentage, calculated by taking runs scored per game (**RS/G**) and runs allowed per game (**RA/G**) for the team, and running them through a version of Bill James' Pythagorean formula that was refined and improved by David Smyth and Brandon Heipp. (The formula is called "Pythagenpat," which is equally fun to type and to say.)

Next up is **DRC+**, described earlier, to indicate the overall hitting ability of the team either above or below league-average. Run prevention on the pitching side is covered by **DRA** (also mentioned earlier) and another metric: Fielding Independent Pitching (**FIP**), which calculates another ERA-like statistic based on strikeouts, walks, and home runs recorded. Defensive Efficiency Rating (**DER**) tells us the percentage of balls in play turned into outs for the team, and is a quick fielding shorthand that rounds out run prevention.

After that, we have several measures related to roster composition, as opposed to on-field performance. **B-Age** and **P-Age** tell us the average age of a team's batters and pitchers, respectively. **Salary** is the combined team payroll for all on-field players, and Doug Pappas' Marginal Dollars per Marginal Win (**M$/MW**) tells us how much money a team spent to earn production above replacement level.

Ending this batch of statistics is the number of disabled list days a team had over the season (**IL Days**) and the amount of salary paid to players on the disabled list (**$ on IL**); this final number is expressed as a percentage of total payroll.

Next to each of these stats, we've listed each team's MLB rank in that category from first to 30th. In this, first always indicates a positive outcome and 30th a negative outcome, except in the case of salary—first is highest.

After the franchise statistics, we share a few items about the team's home ballpark. There's the aforementioned diagram of the park's dimensions (including distances to the outfield wall), a graphic showing the height of the wall from the left-field pole to the right-field pole, and a table showing three-year park factors for the stadium. The park factors are displayed as indexes where 100 is average, 110 means that the park inflates the statistic in question by 10 percent, and 90 means that the park deflates the statistic in question by 10 percent.

On the second page of each team chapter, you'll find three graphs. The first is the **2019 Hit List Ranking**. This shows our Hit List Rank for the team on each day of the 2019 season and is intended to give you a picture of the ups and downs of the team's season. Hit List Rank measures overall team performance and drives the Hit List Power Rankings at the baseballprospectus.com website.

The second graph is **Committed Payroll** and helps you see how the team's payroll has compared to the MLB and divisional average payrolls over time. Payroll figures are current as of January 1, 2020; with so many free agents still unsigned as of this writing, the final 2020 figure will likely be significantly different for many teams. (In the meantime, you can always find the most current data at Baseball Prospectus' Cot's Baseball Contracts page.)

The third graph is **Farm System Ranking** and displays how the Baseball Prospectus prospect team has ranked the organization's farm system since 2007.

After the graphs, we have a **Personnel** section that lists many of the important decision-makers and upper-level field and operations staff members for the franchise, as well as any former Baseball Prospectus staff members who are currently part of the organization. (In very rare circumstances, someone might be on both lists!)

Juan Soto LF
Born: 10/25/98 Age: 21 Bats: L Throws: L
Height: 6'1" Weight: 185 Origin: International Free Agent, 2015

YEAR	TEAM	LVL	AGE	PA	R	2B	3B	HR	RBI	BB	K	SB	CS	AVG/OBP/SLG
2017	NAT	RK	18	27	3	1	1	0	4	2	1	0	0	.320/.370/.440
2017	HAG	A	18	96	15	5	0	3	14	10	8	1	2	.360/.427/.523
2018	HAG	A	19	74	12	5	3	5	24	14	13	2	0	.373/.486/.814
2018	POT	A+	19	73	17	3	1	7	18	11	8	0	1	.371/.466/.790
2018	HAR	AA	19	35	4	2	0	2	10	4	7	1	0	.323/.400/.581
2018	WAS	MLB	19	494	77	25	1	22	70	79	99	5	2	.292/.406/.517
2019	WAS	MLB	20	659	110	32	5	34	110	108	132	12	1	.282/.401/.548
2020	WAS	MLB	21	630	92	30	3	35	102	85	123	5	2	.284/.382/.543

Comparables: Ronald Acuña Jr., Mike Trout, Tony Conigliaro

YEAR	TEAM	LVL	AGE	PA	DRC+	VORP	BABIP	BRR	FRAA	WARP
2017	NAT	RK	18	27	135	1.5	.333	0.0	RF(9): -1.1	0.0
2017	HAG	A	18	96	181	8.0	.373	1.0	RF(19): -1.9, LF(2): -0.3	0.9
2018	HAG	A	19	74	222	14.5	.405	0.3	RF(14): 1.1, CF(2): 0.2	1.2
2018	POT	A+	19	73	260	15.4	.340	1.4	RF(14): 1.0, LF(1): 0.0	1.6
2018	HAR	AA	19	35	113	3.6	.364	0.0	LF(4): 0.6, RF(4): -0.5	0.1
2018	WAS	MLB	19	494	125	40.5	.338	-0.5	LF(114): 2.7	3.0
2019	WAS	MLB	20	659	136	49.0	.312	1.4	LF(150): -0.8	4.9
2020	WAS	MLB	21	630	133	43.6	.310	-0.1	LF 3	4.8

Position Players

After all that information and a thoughtful bylined essay covering each team, we present our player comments. These are also bylined, but due to frequent franchise shifts during the offseason, our bylines are more a rough guide than a perfect accounting of who wrote what.

Each player is listed with the major-league team that employed him as of early January 2020. If a player changed teams after that point via free agency, trade, or any other method, you'll be able to find them in the chapter for their previous squad.

As an example, take a look at the player comment for Nationals outfielder Juan Soto: the stat block that accompanies his written comment is at the top of this page. First we cover biographical information (age is as of June 30, 2020) before moving onto the stats themselves. Our statistic columns include standard identifying information like **YEAR**, **TEAM**, **LVL** (level of affiliated play) and **AGE** before getting into the numbers. Next, we provide raw, untranslated numbers like you might find on the back of your dad's baseball cards: **PA** (plate appearances), **R** (runs), **2B** (doubles), **3B** (triples), **HR** (home runs), **RBI** (runs batted in), **BB** (walks), **K** (strikeouts), **SB** (stolen bases) and **CS** (caught stealing).

Next, we have unadjusted "slash" statistics: **AVG** (batting average), **OBP** (on-base percentage) and **SLG** (slugging percentage). Following the slash line is **DRC+** (Deserved Runs Created Plus), which we described earlier as total offensive expected contribution compared to the league average.

One of our oldest active metrics, **VORP** (Value Over Replacement Player), considers offensive production, position and plate appearances. In essence, it is the number of runs contributed beyond what a replacement-level player at the same position would contribute if given the same percentage of team plate appearances. VORP does not consider the quality of a player's defense.

BABIP (batting average on balls in play) tells us how often a ball in play fell for a hit, and can help us identify whether a batter may have been lucky or not...but note that high BABIPs also tend to follow the great hitters of our time, as well as speedy singles hitters who put the ball on the ground.

The next item is **BRR** (Baserunning Runs), which covers all of a player's baserunning accomplishments including (but not limited to) swiped bags and failed attempts. Next is **FRAA** (Fielding Runs Above Average), which also includes the number of games previously played at each position noted in parentheses. Multi-position players have only their two most frequent positions listed here, but their total FRAA number reflects all positions played.

Our last column here is **WARP** (Wins Above Replacement Player). WARP estimates the total value of a player, which means for hitters it takes into account hitting runs above average (calculated using the DRC+ model), BRR and FRAA. Then, it makes an adjustment for positions played and gives the player a credit for plate appearances based upon the difference between "replacement level"—which is derived from the quality of players added to a team's roster after the start of the season—and the league average.

The final line just below the stats box is **PECOTA** data, which is discussed further in a following section.

Catchers

Catchers are a special breed, and thus they have earned their own separate box which displays some of the defensive metrics that we've built just for them. As an example, let's check out J.T. Realmuto.

The **YEAR** and **TEAM** columns match what you'd find in the other stat box. **P. COUNT** indicates the number of pitches thrown while the catcher was behind the plate, including swinging strikes, fouls and balls in play. **FRM RUNS** is the total run value the catcher provided (or cost) his team by influencing the umpire to call strikes where other catchers did not. **BLK RUNS** expresses the total run value above or below average for the catcher's ability to prevent wild pitches and passed balls. **THRW RUNS** is calculated using a similar model as the previous two statistics, and it measures a catcher's ability to throw out basestealers but also to dissuade them from testing his arm in the first place. It takes into account factors like the pitcher (including his delivery and pickoff move) and baserunner (who could be as fast as Billy Hamilton or as slow as Yonder Alonso). **TOT RUNS** is the sum of all of the previous three statistics.

Justin Verlander   RHP
Born: 02/20/83   Age: 37   Bats: R   Throws: R
Height: 6'5"   Weight: 225   Origin: Round 1, 2004 Draft (#2 overall)

YEAR	TEAM	LVL	AGE	W	L	SV	G	GS	IP	H	HR	BB/9	K/9	K	GB%	BABIP
2017	DET	MLB	34	10	8	0	28	28	172	153	23	3.5	9.2	176	34%	.283
2017	HOU	MLB	34	5	0	0	5	5	34	17	4	1.3	11.4	43	32%	.194
2018	HOU	MLB	35	16	9	0	34	34	214	156	28	1.6	12.2	290	31%	.272
2019	HOU	MLB	36	21	6	0	34	34	223	137	36	1.7	12.1	300	36%	.219
2020	HOU	MLB	37	15	6	0	29	29	184	138	28	2.3	12.1	248	35%	.274

Comparables: Zack Greinke, A.J. Burnett, Aníbal Sánchez

YEAR	TEAM	LVL	AGE	WHIP	ERA	DRA	WARP	MPH	FB%	WHF	CSP
2017	DET	MLB	34	1.28	3.82	4.03	3.0	97.7	58	11	47.8
2017	HOU	MLB	34	0.65	1.06	3.08	0.9	97.5	59.6	15.1	49.9
2018	HOU	MLB	35	0.90	2.52	2.33	7.3	97.5	61.2	16.2	51.6
2019	HOU	MLB	36	0.80	2.58	2.51	7.9	96.8	49.9	17.5	48.3
2020	HOU	MLB	37	1.01	2.75	2.95	5.3	95.8	54.6	15.1	48.2

Pitchers

Let's give our pitchers a turn, using 2019 AL Cy Young winner Justin Verlander as our example. Take a look at his stat block: the first line and the **YEAR**, **TEAM**, **LVL** and **AGE** columns are the same as in the position player example earlier.

Here too, we have a series of columns that display raw, unadjusted statistics compiled by the pitcher over the course of a season: **W** (wins), **L** (losses), **SV** (saves), **G** (games pitched), **GS** (games started), **IP** (innings pitched), **H** (hits allowed) and **HR** (home runs allowed). Next we have two statistics that are rates: **BB/9** (walks per nine innings) and **K/9** (strikeouts per nine innings), before returning to the unadjusted K (strikeouts).

Next up is **GB%** (ground ball percentage), which is the percentage of all batted balls that were hit on the ground, including both outs and hits. Remember, this is based on observational data and subject to human error, so please approach this with a healthy dose of skepticism.

BABIP (batting average on balls in play) is calculated using the same methodology as it is for position players, but it often tells us more about a pitcher than it does a hitter. With pitchers, a high BABIP is often due to poor defense or bad luck, and can often be an indicator of potential rebound, and a low BABIP may be cause to expect performance regression. (A typical league-average BABIP is close to .290-.300.)

Los Angeles Dodgers 2020

The metrics **WHIP** (walks plus hits per inning pitched) and **ERA** (earned run average) are old standbys: WHIP measures walks and hits allowed on a per-inning basis, while ERA measures earned runs on a nine-inning basis. Neither of these stats are translated or adjusted.

DRA (Deserved Run Average) was described at length earlier, and measures how many runs the pitcher "deserved" to allow per nine innings. Please note that since we lack all the data points that would make for a "real" DRA for minor-league events, the DRA displayed for minor league partial-seasons is based off of different data. (That data is a modified version of our cFIP metric, which you can find more information about on our website.)

Just like with hitters, **WARP** (Wins Above Replacement Player) is a total value metric that puts pitchers of all stripes on the same scale as position players. We use DRA as the primary input for our calculation of WARP. You might notice that relief pitchers (due to their limited innings) may have a lower WARP than you were expecting or than you might see in other WARP-like metrics. WARP does not take leverage into account, just the actions a pitcher performs and the expected value of those actions...which ends up judging high-leverage relief pitchers differently than you might imagine given their prestige and market value.

MPH gives you the pitcher's 95th percentile velocity for the noted season, in order to give you an idea of what the *peak* fastball velocity a pitcher possesses. Since this comes from our pitch-tracking data, it is not publicly available for minor-league pitchers.

Finally, we display the three new pitching metrics we described earlier. **FB%** (fastball percentage) gives you the percentage of fastballs thrown out of all pitches. **WHF** (whiff rate) tells you the percentage of swinging strikes induced out of all pitches. **CSP** (called strike probability) expresses the likelihood of all pitches thrown to result in a called strike, after controlling for factors like handedness, umpire, pitch type, count and location.

PECOTA

All players have PECOTA projections for 2020, as well as a set of other numbers that describe the performance of comparable players according to PECOTA. All projections for 2020 are for the player at the date we went to press in early January and are projected into the league and park context as indicated by the team abbreviation. (Note that players at very low levels of the minors are too unpredictable to assess using these numbers.) All PECOTA projected statistics represent a player's projected major-league performance.

Below the projections are the player's three highest-scoring comparable players as determined by PECOTA. All comparables represent a snapshot of how the listed player was performing at the same age as the current player, so if a

23-year-old pitcher is compared to Bartolo Colón, he's actually being compared to a 23-year-old Colón, not the version that pitched for the Rangers in 2018, nor to Colón's career as a whole.

A few points about pitcher projections. First, we aren't yet projecting peak velocity, so that column will be blank in the PECOTA lines. Second, projecting DRA is trickier than evaluating past performance, because it is unclear how deserving each pitcher will be of his anticipated outcomes. However, we know that another DRA-related statistic–contextual FIP or cFIP-estimates future run scoring very well. So for PECOTA, the projected DRA figures you see are based on the past cFIPs generated by the pitcher and comparable players over time, along with the other factors described above.

Lineouts

In each chapter's Lineouts section, you'll find abbreviated text comments, as well as all the same information you'd find in our full player comments. The only difference is that we limit the stats boxes in this section to only including the 2019 information for each player.

Managers

After all those wonderful team chapters, we've got statistics for each big-league manager, all of whom are organized by alphabetical order. Here you'll find a block including an extraordinary amount of information collected from each manager's entire career. For more information on the acronyms and what they mean, please visit the Glossary at www.baseballprospectus.com.

There is one important metric that we'd like to call attention to, and you'll find it next to each manager's name: **wRM+** (weighted reliever management plus). Developed by Rob Arthur and Rian Watt, wRM+ investigates how good a manager is at using their best relievers during the moments of highest leverage, using both our proprietary DRA metric as well as Leverage Index. wRM+ is scaled to a league average of 100, and a wRM+ of 105 indicates that relievers were used approximately five percent "better" than average. On the other hand, a wRM+ of 95 would tell us the team used its relievers five percent "worse" than the average team.

While wRM+ does not have an extremely strong correlation with a manager, it is statistically significant; this means that a manager is not *entirely* responsible for a team's wRM+, but does have some effect on that number.

PECOTA Leaderboards

If you're familiar with PECOTA, then you'll have noticed that the projection system often appears bullish on players coming off a bad year and bearish on players coming off a good year. (This is because the system weights several previous seasons, not just the most recent one.) In addition, we publish the 50th

Los Angeles Dodgers 2020

percentile projections for each player–which is smack in the middle of the range of projected production—which tends to mean PECOTA stat lines don't often have extreme results like 40 home runs or 250 strikeouts in a given season. In essence, PECOTA doesn't project very many extreme seasons.

At the end of the book, we've ranked the top players at each position based on their PECOTA projections. This might help you visualize just how a given player's projection compares to that of their peers, so that even if a dramatic stat line isn't projected, you can still imagine how they stack up against the rest of the league.

xvi - Statistical Introduction

Part 1: Team Analysis

Los Angeles Dodgers: Where Are You Going, Where Have You Been?

Craig Goldstein, Jeffrey Paternostro and Matthew Trueblood

2019: What Went Right

Heading into the season, expectations were high for the Dodgers. With back-to-back trips to the World Series on their resume but no trophy decorated with flags to show for it, anything but a dominant division title would be considered a failure. Fail they did not; the team opened up a nine-game lead by June 1 and never really looked back en route to a franchise-record 106-win season and the best record in the National League.

A lot has to go right for a team to win 106 games, and for the Dodgers that started with Cody Bellinger. The first baseman-cum-right fielder-cum-center fielder excelled at every position they could slot him in, compiling 10 outfield assists on the way to a 15.4 FRAA. As good as he is with the leather, Bellinger was better with the stick. His 158 DRC+ ranked third in the major leagues, and second in the National League, trailing only Christian Yelich. A taller stance and a tighter zone drove his walk rate up three percentage points while he lopped 7.5 percentage points off his strikeout rate. The increased selectivity and contact meant that when he did connect, it was loud. Forty-seven home runs, 115 RBI and 15 stolen bases later, he was deservedly voted the NL MVP.

Hyun-Jin Ryu essentially matched Bellinger in quality in the first half of the season, flummoxing the league with a five-pitch mix that deceived more than dazzled. He leaned heavily on a changeup that baffles hitters because he sells it so well with his arm speed, and in so doing earned both a lot of weak contact and a start in the All-Star Game. He couldn't replicate his 1.73 ERA in the second half, but he still ended the season with the first black ink on his resume thanks to a 2.32 ERA and 1.2 walks-per-nine.

Max Muncy proved he wasn't a one-year wonder with a second straight season of 35 homers, although his DRC+ dropped from 146 to 131 in the process. Still, five-win seasons aren't particularly easy to come by unless you're a retread signing with the Dodgers.

Walker Buehler took the next step in his maturation process, and while Ryu had the best year and Clayton Kershaw is the living legend, it is Buehler who is the ace of the staff. He upped his innings total without losing quality, churning out an almost-six-win season on the back of a 29 percent strikeout rate and a 2.89 DRA. Kershaw took a streak of at least six-plus innings pitched in every start into the 20s and stayed healthy the whole season. He recorded a 3.03 ERA, the first time he's finished a season with an ERA over 3.00 since 2008, his rookie year. Still, health is paramount for Kershaw, though his consistency over the course of the season belied first-inning struggles and some inconsistency in his slider depth.

Catcher was perhaps the weakest position on the roster: Though both backstops have their talents behind the plate, rotating between an ineffective Austin Barnes and a passive Russell Martin at the dish was suboptimal. Will Smith (no, not that one...the baseball one...no, the other baseball one) came to the rescue in the second half of the season. Long-mentioned as trade bait, Smith arrived and scored positive numbers defensively to go with a .571 slugging percentage—good for second among all catchers with a minimum of 100 plate appearances. You may have noticed but catchers who can frame and hit don't come along too often.

There are a smattering of other successful if unremarkable aspects of the rest of the Dodgers season. Joc Pederson continued murdering pull-side fly balls, Corey Seager stroked a lot of doubles when he wasn't missing time with various injuries, Justin Turner played in 135 games and performed as he always does, David Freese had a 1.002 OPS in limited playing time. There was a cavalcade of rookies who came up and performed anywhere from adequately to admirably: Alex Verdugo hit close to .300 before getting hurt, Gavin Lux flashed in his September call-up, Edwin Ríos absolutely mashed, Matt Beaty looked like at least a platoon guy going forward, and Dustin May and Tony Gonsolin both played significant roles down the stretch. Even Kyle Garlick got in on the action, with an .842 OPS in limited time. Hell, in one three-game series with Colorado, the team received walk-off hits from three different rookies (Will Smith, Kyle Garlick, Matt Beaty). May looked a lot like Waluigi that one time he chased a foul ball.

2019: What Went Wrong

Eschewing the top of the free agent market during the 2018-2019 offseason, the Dodgers settled for A.J. Pollock in an attempt to stay under the luxury tax for a second consecutive year, just what every fan wants. Pollock was...okay. He was also injured—big surprise—and then flamed out spectacularly in the playoffs going 0-13 with 11 strikeouts and one walk. What's cooler than being cool?

The trade deadline was reminiscent of Pollock in the playoffs; it was another swing and a miss. While many elite bullpen options were bandied about, Andrew Friedman and company didn't land their big fish. Fortunately, it wouldn't come back to haunt them, no, not at all. …Okay, so we have to talk about it, I guess. The NLDS went…well, wrong feels like an understatement. It went heinously, egregiously, soul-shatteringly wrong. While the Nationals were probably the second-best National League team in the playoffs, it shouldn't have even come to this. The Nats used both of their best pitchers in the Wild Card game, so there should have been an advantage in facing either their lesser arms (Aníbal Sánchez) or tired ones. Alas and alack. Corey Seager struggled to a .390 OPS in 20 at-bats. Bellinger wasn't much better at .549 in 19. Will Smith checked in at .327 in 13 at-bats. Chris Taylor went 1-8. The team as a whole hit .135/.340/.351 with runners in scoring position in the series. Game 5 (and no small part of Game 4) rests on the shoulders of Dave Roberts. That it even got to that point rests on no small number of players who underperformed. —*Craig Goldstein*

Prospect Outlook

The Dodgers continue to supplement their major-league roster with an above-average farm system. Last season saw the major league debuts of Dustin May and Gavin Lux, both of whom are still list-eligible and elite prospects regardless of service time. May could slot into the Dodgers rotation as soon as Opening Day 2020 and has top-of-the-rotation upside if he can hone his cutter and power curve a bit more. Lux had a breakout season, blitzing the upper minors to the tune of a 1.000 OPS. He's ready to man a spot in the middle infield in 2020, and it's hard to find a weakness anywhere in his overall tools profile. It's hard to find anything worse than average.

The Dodgers system is strong at the top, but it also runs deep. You could easily find 25 prospects here with potential major-league futures better than "extra bench guy." **Keibert Ruiz** had an uneven 2019 campaign but remains one of the best catching prospects in baseball. **Josiah Gray**—acquired in the Yasiel Puig deal—could be their next breakout arm, and the other piece of that trade, **Jeter Downs**, had a strong A-ball campaign as well. Either could be on the cusp of major-league utility by late this year. It was certainly a disappointing end to the Dodgers' 2019, but the future remains bright. —*Jeffrey Paternostro*

2020 Outlook

No fan of an Andrew Friedman-led team ever need worry that he'll miss an opportunity to pounce on a great value. Friedman (and the high-powered front office he builds around him) is extremely thorough and detail-oriented. Trades with the Braves and Reds in each of the last two offseasons, ostensibly structured solely to thread the team's luxury-tax needle, are shining examples of the way he finds the best available version of the move he needs to make.

However, Friedman is also exceptionally value-conscious, which is why he's rarely seen holding one sleeve of a jersey at a press conference. That trend continued in the winter of 2019-20, even with pressure to get the Dodgers over the hump mounting. The previous two free-agent markets, which developed so slowly and held prices down so efficiently, made the Dodgers willing to go from dipping their toes into the deep end to sitting on the edge of the pool and dangling their lower legs, but they didn't take the dive—not with Gerrit Cole, and not with Anthony Rendon. The financial terms just weren't attractive enough to the L.A. front office, given their low level of real need.

As January slogged toward its conclusion, however, that occasional opportunity came, and Friedman got his men. The Red Sox were hemmed in by ownership pressure to get back underneath the tax threshold, and their leverage in negotiations on a Mookie Betts trade evaporated. Friedman did his own fancy trade footwork, shipping Kenta Maeda and Alex Verdugo (along with prospects Downs and Connor Wong) out of town to make room on the roster, but he landed Betts and David Price, turning the Dodgers into a super team (if they weren't one already). It was classic Friedman, but with plenty of Hollywood flair. Betts gives the Dodgers the best, deepest, and most exciting lineup in baseball. Price gives them, more or less, what Maeda was giving them: stability in a rotation slot they treat as a small cog in a big pitching machine. —*Matthew Trueblood*

Performance Graphs

2019 Hit List Ranking

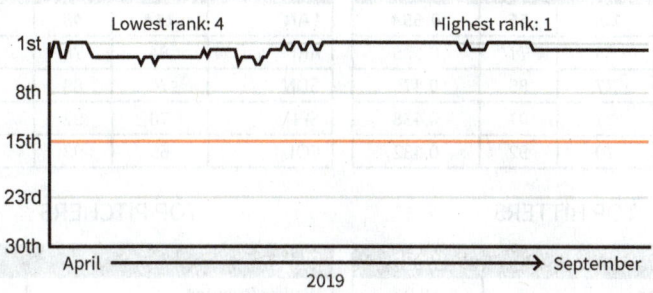

Committed Payroll (in millions)

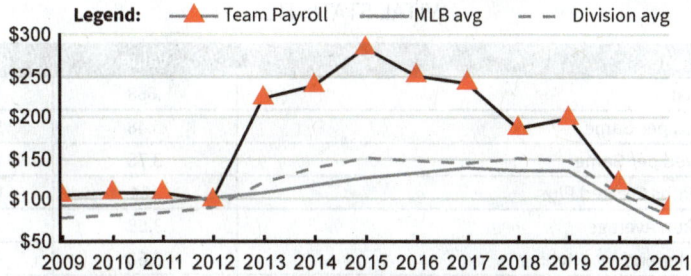

Farm System Ranking

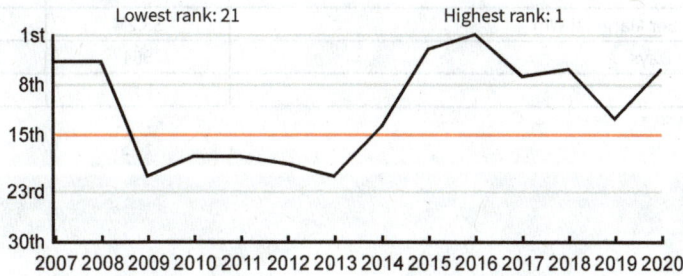

2019 Team Performance

ACTUAL STANDINGS

Team	W	L	Pct
LAN	106	56	0.654
ARI	85	77	0.525
SFN	77	85	0.475
COL	71	91	0.438
SDN	70	92	0.432

THIRD-ORDER STANDINGS

Team	W	L	Pct
LAN	114	48	0.702
ARI	84	78	0.516
SDN	74	88	0.454
SFN	70	92	0.431
COL	69	93	0.429

TOP HITTERS

Player	WARP
Cody Bellinger	8.0
Max Muncy	5.1
Justin Turner	4.5

TOP PITCHERS

Player	WARP
Walker Buehler	5.7
Hyun-Jin Ryu	5.4
Clayton Kershaw	4.7

VITAL STATISTICS

Statistic Name	Value	Rank
Pythagenpat	.668	1st
Runs Scored per Game	5.48	5th
Runs Allowed per Game	3.78	1st
Deserved Runs Created Plus	104	6th
Deserved Run Average	3.58	1st
Fielding Independent Pitching	3.68	1st
Defensive Efficiency Rating	.729	1st
Batter Age	27.8	12th
Pitcher Age	28.8	22nd
Salary	$196.3M	5th
Marginal $ per Marginal Win	$3.2M	20th
Injured List Days	964	10th
$ on IL	12%	7th

2020 Team Projections

PROJECTED STANDINGS

Team	W	L	Pct	+/-
LAN	102.5	59.5	0.633	-4
SDN	79.3	82.7	0.490	9
ARI	78.9	83.1	0.487	-6
COL	76.6	85.4	0.473	6
SFN	68.4	93.6	0.422	-9

TOP PROJECTED HITTERS

Player	WARP
Mookie Betts	6.6
Cody Bellinger	4.9
Will Smith	3.6

TOP PROJECTED PITCHERS

Player	WARP
Clayton Kershaw	5.5
Walker Buehler	4.7
David Price	2.2

FARM SYSTEM REPORT

Top Prospect	Number of Top 101 Prospects
Gavin Lux, #3	6

KEY DEDUCTIONS

Player	WARP
Kenta Maeda	2.8
Hyun-Jin Ryu	2.4
Alex Verdugo	1.9
Yimi García	0.8
Rich Hill	0.5
Jedd Gyorko	0.2
Casey Sadler	0.0
Kyle Garlick	-0.1

KEY ADDITIONS

Player	WARP
Mookie Betts	6.6
David Price	2.2
Alex Wood	0.9
Luke Raley	0.8
Blake Treinen	0.6
Zach McKinstry	0.1
Josiah Gray	0.1
Mitchell White	0.1
Jimmy Nelson	0.1
Edubray Ramos	0.0

Team Personnel

President, Baseball Operations
Andrew Friedman

Senior Vice President, Baseball Operations
Josh Byrnes

Vice President & Assistant General Manager
Brandon Gomes

Vice President & Assistant General Manager
Jeffrey Kingston

Manager
Dave Roberts

BP Alumni
Ricky Conti

Dodger Stadium Stats

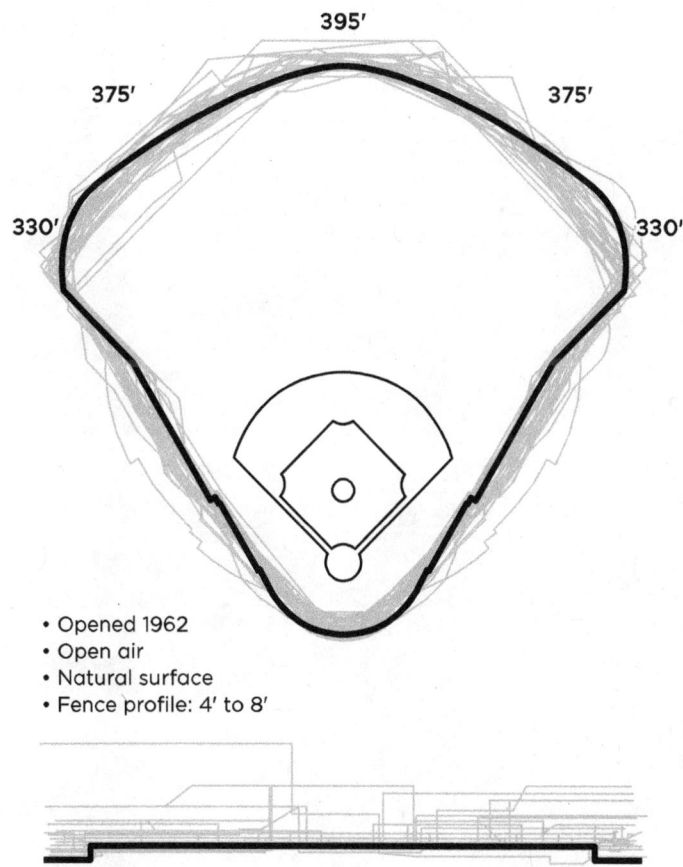

- Opened 1962
- Open air
- Natural surface
- Fence profile: 4' to 8'

Three-Year Park Factors

Runs	Runs/RH	Runs/LH	HR/RH	HR/LH
96	95	100	104	107

Dodgers Team Analysis

It was an ugly swing, a swing like a rough shove in a bar fight, and as Cody Bellinger ranged back he looked up every two steps, as if expecting it to die. His long stride stretched into an elope, as if his feet were caught in the slow-motion of the moment, as if he would keep running halfway to the wall forever, as in a dream. And then his hands slapped the blue vinyl just as the ball sailed overhead and, in an instant, the work of eight months, of 106 wins, of perhaps the most talented Dodgers team in history dissolved on camera, a supercut of hollow stares into some other timeline before fading into black. The fans pulsed up the aisles as though the stadium itself were bleeding out blue.

Baseball is designed to be fair and unfair. The physics of the bat and ball generates, more than any other action in professional sports, pure chaos; it bends but does not break to the strongest manipulation of reason and strategy. It's the mythology that rejects mythology, propping up nobodies and felling heroes. It cuts down demigods like Clayton Kershaw and props up the likes of Howie Kendrick. It gives us teams like the Los Angeles Dodgers, winners of more games this decade than any other NL franchise, perched alongside such dynasties as the 1960s Giants, the 1970s Red Sox, and the 1990s Mariners, the incomplete elite.

After the loss, after destiny swept their opponents to their ensuing championship, the message was clear: Something had to change. The Nationals, as the symbol for modern postseason futility, are no more; now, the Dodgers are the Nationals. Seven years of beautiful summers and grisly autumns were enough. As of printing, that change hasn't happened yet. The team's transactions as of the end of the year amounted to signing one reliever on a bounce-back contract, even as they suffered the loss of Hyun-Jin Ryu and Rich Hill. On offense, there are more reinforcements than holes to patch, as Will Smith, Gavin Lux and Alex Verdugo demonstrated that the machine is still firing on all cylinders. And yet for a fanbase in need of postseason heroics, there are no new heroes, no deck chairs to shuffle. The Dodgers were never designed to change, but then, they weren't designed to lose.

It's difficult to evaluate a ballclub so consistently successful and disappointing; it resists traditional analysis. Besides, number crunching always fails to capture the dualism of the sport, thirty nation-states that act as both teams and corporations. So instead we'll apply the lens of military philosophy. In his book *Just and Unjust Wars*, professor Henry Walzer divides the ethics of war into two categories: *jus in bello* and *jus ad bellum*. The first belongs to the hemisphere of justice within war: what is considered acceptable behavior during battle. This includes the war convention and its rules: don't use mustard gas, don't shoot soldiers after they've surrendered, leave the ambulance drivers alone. The second centers on the justice of going to war, or when it's acceptable to bear arms at all, to invade, to strike first. The goal of the exercise is not to grade a particular team, but to prove that ethics are both possible and attainable, that wars can be limited, and games can be played fair.

And in a strange way, the story of the 2019 Dodgers isn't even about the 2019 season. Stories always begin before their beginnings. This one starts half a century ago on the other side of the country, and marches toward its resolution in the ruins of a recent battlefield: The hollow irregular timpani ring of a trash can that not one person heard, and now echoes everywhere.

⚾   ⚾   ⚾

Baseball is hardly war, and we're spared the worst of the clichés so often anointed upon the ugly phalanx thrust that is football. Like any sport, though, baseball isn't totally divorced from war, either: The *Iliad* caps its history of the Trojan War not with the death of Hektor or the retrieval of Helen, but with a postwar chariot race that mends the alliances of the victorious army. Athletic contest has always served as both a training ground and a psychological substitute for armed conflict, a channeling of social aggression. In an America that grows increasingly culturally homogenous in the age of the internet and Amazon, professional sports hold as one of the last remaining vestiges of localized nationalism, even in Los Angeles, the city that exports so much of that homogeneity to the world.

The Spartans employed sports to train their warriors, get them used to grappling and spears, but they also served as their cultural indoctrination, a rite of passage. Today, sports take on a more moderate application of these same ideals, the intent being to build character, discipline, teamwork and sportsmanship. Baseball, at its heart, is a code of ethics: It's an amalgam of intricate, incomprehensible rules specifying human conduct to an inhuman degree, rivaling Leviticus, with another invisible code laid on top of it by the tradition of the players themselves. One of its core tenets is the shared, level playing field, the equal opportunity it provides each man. The game is at heart a contract, a social construct, and it only works when everyone adheres to its values in good faith.

Justice within war, *jus in bello*, maps onto baseball's rules, written and unwritten: Don't run too far outside the lines. Don't gamble on your sport. Don't throw the ball at a batter's head, and don't hit John Roseboro in the head with a bat. The Dodgers have generally, since their arrival in Los Angeles, taken on the aura of good-natured, clean-playing young men, almost as if the climate were baked into them. It took shape in the '70s, with Rick Monday saving the flag and imperturbable Steve Garvey fielding reporters; it carried through the officious and efficient Orel Hershiser and holds today, despite the bat flips of Yasiel Puig and the blood drawn by the errant cleats of Chase Utley and Manny Machado. It's not an ethos of grit, no Cardinals Way, but rather just the languorous ease of conspicuous talent. The Dodgers have three losing seasons in a quarter of a century, almost despite themselves at times. They ascend beyond grit.

After the installation of Andrew Friedman as President of Baseball Operations, the destiny of the Dodgers seemed almost foregone. It culminated in a 2017 team that fell a game shy of ending the team's three-decade championship drought. It was perhaps the most exciting, evenly-matched final in memory, the battle of two model franchises at the peak of their power. The Astros won, because in sports, unlike war, someone has to win. They also, as it turns out, cheated.

The news came out just this offseason, by way of the testimony of four people, including former Astro Mike Fiers: An intricate and institutional system for stealing and relaying signs was in place for the entire 2017 season. The Astros used a camera in center field to read the catcher's signs, and employees and players in the clubhouse tunnel deciphered them, and banged on a nearby trash can to tell the batter that an offspeed was coming. As Rob Arthur analyzed at Baseball Prospectus, the correlation of trash can signals and strikeouts at Minute Maid on pitches in the dirt was decisive. MLB has begun an investigation into the accusations, though video and correspondence have already demonstrated a damning level of proof. As the book heads to print, MLB's decision, and its potential punishment, have not been established.

One takeaway seems safe to publish: Rob Manfred may make the Astros organization regret the choices they made, but it will be of little use to fans in Los Angeles. Even in the NCAA, a vacated title doesn't find a new home; it just never happened. But such a result is itself unthinkably drastic, and it's more likely to result in fines, draft pick forfeitures, and/or suspensions. The flag will fly forever, no matter how blackened. Such is war; chemical weapons are prohibited by the war convention, but the world has no real commissioner. Tribunals are powerless to bring back the dead, and mournful bells can't be unrung.

⚾ ⚾ ⚾

So the Dodgers were victims of a violation of the rules of engagement in 2017. More meaningful to the current roster is the other half of the equation. *Jus ad bellum* is the trickier aspect to translate to baseball, because it regards the justice of when to go to war, when to make a political act guaranteed to kill people. There are no such aggressions in baseball because it's a sport that exists in continual (mock) conflict. So perhaps the better way to define the justice of baseball, as nation-states rather than individual combatants, is to examine whether a team is acting ethically based on the customs of the sport itself: Are the Dodgers behaving the way that a baseball team ought to behave?

There are two ways to answer this question, because baseball is an interconnected relationship between three parties: the team, the players, and the fans. In terms of the team's conduct with its players, the record isn't quite as sun-dappled as its on-field reputation. The team remains under investigation by the U.S. Department of Justice for its documented involvement in the shady world of international scouting, including official interaction with *buscones*, local agents whose interests often align with human trafficking and organized crime. It's a widespread issue across the league, but the Dodgers figure prominently because of the existence of an internal document, a "crimes.xlsx," that lists the names of team employees and an estimation—on a scale of 1 to 5—how their behavior ranks, from "innocent bystander" to "criminal."

Also unresolved is the conduct of former head of player development and current San Francisco Giants manager Gabe Kapler, who in 2015 was notified of sexual assault committed by a Dodgers minor leaguer against a 17-year-old. Kapler insisted that he hadn't been made aware of the incident. It was later revealed via a *Sports Illustrated* report that this was not true; not only had he chosen not to notify the police of the crime, he failed to enlist any professional help in his attempt to resolve the matter internally. The situation speaks to a lack of institutional control, and accountability, over the conditions of the team's employees.

Assessing the ethics of the Dodgers' conduct toward its fans is a more difficult task. One of the primary causes for concern in the modern era of baseball is the transition of its revenue, away from ticket sales toward a greater influence of broadcast media and merchandising. The sport is, in a way, too popular for its own good, and it is too easy for corporations in this strange, restricted trust to extract money from its fans. For a century, baseball teams had two ways to profit: win, or develop players and sell them to winners. True, social mobility was often nonexistent, and the bottom feeders of the league could never quite get ahead. But profit was tied to winning, and winning meant selling tickets. Today, that correlation no longer holds true: baseball teams no longer have to sell out to make money. They make money, as each new sale proves, just by existing, as the last money market accounts on earth.

The Dodgers do draw—half a million more than the second-place Cardinals, and five times as many fans as the Marlins—and they do offer a product worth watching. The team understands this, of course, and has responded by raising prices to meet demand. Bill Shaikin of the *Los Angeles Times* recently reported that, a family of four will pay, on average, around $150 for the privilege of sitting in the cheap seats. That's half of the median L.A. family's discretionary spending for the entire month, devoted to a single Rockies game. Sports franchises across the country have been converting the stadium experience of baseball into a luxury event, and in so doing have priced out its poorer, and younger, audience. Couple that with the ongoing price war over cable television that has left half the city unable to watch a Dodgers game, and it's easy to see why the team feels so isolated and foreign to even its hometown fans.

The other violation of the contract between the Dodgers and their fans, however, is the allocation of those revenues. Despite its massive income, for the third straight offseason the team refused to go over the luxury tax threshold, despite public statements that the decision was not a mandate from ownership. There are plenty of terms for explaining this kind of fiscal conservatism—payroll flexibility is in vogue—but they're meaningless. The Dodgers have chosen to enter the 2020 season with a roster that, especially on the pitching side, appears weaker than the one that lost to the Nationals. The rotation depth that has marked the Andrew Friedman era has been worn away, and an injury or two could leave the 2020 Dodgers in perilous condition. Given their resources, it's an unjustifiable risk. Unless you're a shareholder.

⚾ ⚾ ⚾

This, then, is the Dodgers' crime, every bit as great as the one laid against them by Houston. We expect sportsmanship out of players, but we must demand equal sportsmanship out of teams. The violation of *jus in bello* on the level of the Houston Astros is something that should and will be punished, severely. But the Dodgers, as an organization, are hardly without guilt. On the level of *jus ad bellum*, this means that every team must try not just to profit, but to win, and must use all the resources available to them in order to do so.

Cheating has been a part of baseball since its inception, and the way in which the game governs itself and interprets its lawbreakers is a strange and obscure process. Stealing signs from second is fine, if done subtly, while doing it through binoculars or cameras or watches is not. What matters isn't the law itself, it's the unquestionable faith of everyone involved, players and teams and fans, that the process is fair, and conducted in good faith. It's the same as war; nations avoid committing atrocities because they don't want the global repercussions, but also because they don't want to have those same atrocities committed against them later. Everyone benefits from fair, limited war, and fair baseball.

Somewhere along the path from childhood to adulthood, sportsmanship evaporates from organized baseball. In fact, the intricate moral system created to house baseball does the opposite of instilling values in its players. Instead, it frees it from them entirely. No professional athlete, after a questionable call comes down in their favor, turns to the umpire and admits, "Actually, I'm pretty sure I was out." It's the umpire's job to make the call, and thus the player is freed from all obligation. And by extension, all cheating is the responsibility of the judges to catch. "It's only cheating if you get caught" is a worn baseball cliché, but what it fails to explain is: if you do get caught, so what?

The what, ultimately, is that the entire sport suffers. The Los Angeles Dodgers, with their legacy, their fanbase and their player development, are perhaps the league's model franchise, for good and for ill. It's easy to imagine them, one year from now, the champions of baseball; it's equally easy to envision them tarnishing the league. Ultimately it will come down to how they fight, and what they fight for. ■

—Patrick Dubuque is an author of Baseball Prospectus.

Part 2: Player Analysis

PLAYER COMMENTS WITH GRAPHS

Matt Beaty   OF/1B
Born: 04/28/93   Age: 27   Bats: L   Throws: R
Height: 6'0"   Weight: 215   Origin: Round 12, 2015 Draft (#372 overall)

YEAR	TEAM	LVL	AGE	PA	R	2B	3B	HR	RBI	BB	K	SB	CS	AVG/OBP/SLG
2017	TUL	AA	24	481	61	31	1	15	69	35	54	3	3	.326/.378/.505
2018	OKL	AAA	25	120	13	10	0	1	12	12	17	0	0	.277/.378/.406
2019	OKL	AAA	26	135	17	7	1	3	18	10	12	0	0	.306/.378/.455
2019	LAN	MLB	26	268	36	19	1	9	46	17	33	5	0	.265/.317/.458
2020	LAN	MLB	27	84	9	5	0	3	10	5	12	0	0	.259/.313/.421

Comparables: Gordy Coleman, José Osuna, Tim Locastro

Batt Meaty started out as a convenient spoonerism, but ended up being an appropriate description of his breakout 2019. Drafted out of college, Beaty was 24 when he made it to Double-A and he was never ranked as a relevant prospect by any publication. Yet he continued to hit, putting up a .309/.367/.447 slash line in the minors, and injuries to the veteran Dodgers gave him a chance to prove he could do it in the majors as well. After a scorching start, Beaty cooled off and finished the year with a below-average DRC+ over 268 plate appearances. It won't wow anyone, but to get a credible utility man from a 12th-round pick—who earned starts in the NLDS—speaks to the job the organization's player development program has done. Normally Beaty would be a candidate for regression back towards something like organizational depth, but betting against a Dodgers hitter who has shown quality development comes with a warning label at this point.

YEAR	TEAM	LVL	AGE	PA	DRC+	VORP	BABIP	BRR	FRAA	WARP
2017	TUL	AA	24	481	158	32.6	.343	0.2	1B(55): 2.3, 3B(49): -0.7	3.9
2018	OKL	AAA	25	120	109	5.3	.321	-0.3	1B(16): -0.3, LF(5): 1.0	0.5
2019	OKL	AAA	26	135	92	6.9	.321	-0.4	1B(11): -0.9, 3B(11): 1.4	0.3
2019	LAN	MLB	26	268	94	4.5	.275	1.1	1B(35): -0.7, LF(34): 0.6	0.5
2020	LAN	MLB	27	84	93	1.8	.277	0.1	LF 1	0.3

Matt Beaty, continued

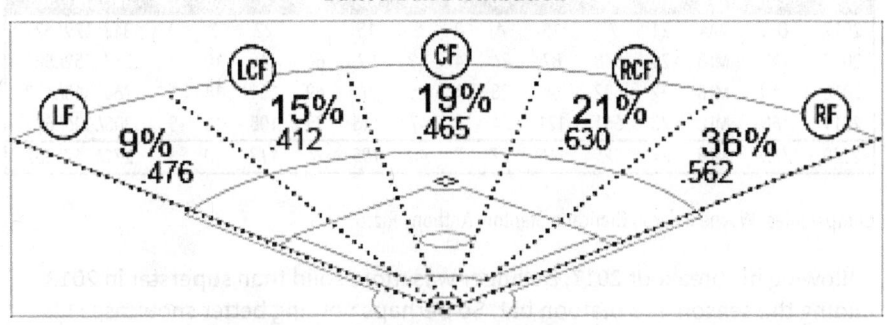

Batted Ball Distribution

| Strike Zone vs LHP | Strike Zone vs RHP |

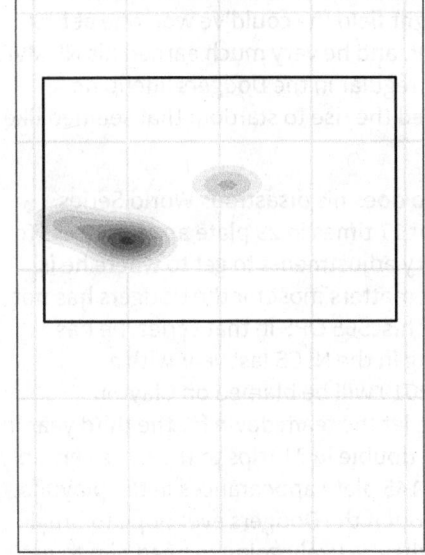 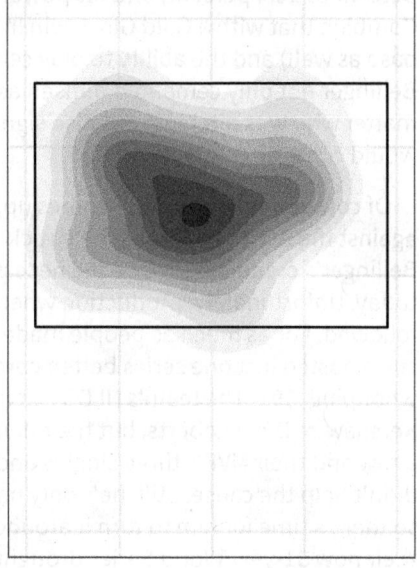

Los Angeles Dodgers 2020

Cody Bellinger OF/1B
Born: 07/13/95   Age: 24   Bats: L   Throws: L
Height: 6'4"   Weight: 203   Origin: Round 4, 2013 Draft (#124 overall)

YEAR	TEAM	LVL	AGE	PA	R	2B	3B	HR	RBI	BB	K	SB	CS	AVG/OBP/SLG
2017	OKL	AAA	21	77	15	4	0	5	15	9	22	7	0	.343/.429/.627
2017	LAN	MLB	21	548	87	26	4	39	97	64	146	10	3	.267/.352/.581
2018	LAN	MLB	22	632	84	28	7	25	76	69	151	14	1	.260/.343/.470
2019	LAN	MLB	23	661	121	34	3	47	115	95	108	15	5	.305/.406/.629
2020	LAN	MLB	24	595	91	27	2	40	105	76	113	10	3	.271/.367/.562

Comparables: Wayne Belardi, Giancarlo Stanton, Anthony Rizzo

Following his breakout 2017, Bellinger was more solid than superstar in 2018, ending the season as a platoon bat. So perhaps nothing better showcases his ascent in 2019 than his OPS boost from .681 to .982 against southpaws, powering his overall 1.035 OPS. But that's just the start, as his walk rate improved (10.9 percent to 14.4 percent), his strikeout rate plummeted (23.9 percent to 16.4 percent) and his power busted loose (60 XBH to 84 XBH). Combine that with a Gold Glove win in right field (he could've won one at first base as well) and the ability to play center, and he very much earned his NL MVP. Bellinger not only cemented himself as a regular in the Dodgers lineup no matter who was pitching, but also signified the rise to stardom that seemed like would come after 2017.

Of course, whenever 2017 comes up, so does his disastrous World Series against the Astros—in which he struck out 17 times in 29 plate appearances. To Bellinger's credit, he's made the necessary adjustments to get to where he is today. Unfortunately, production when it matters most for the Dodgers has not followed. For as much as people made of his .565 OPS in that series, he has since posted just one series better, coming in the NLCS last year with a whopping .591. The team's NLDS exit in 2019 will be blamed on Clayton Kershaw or Dave Roberts, but the offense let the team down for the third year in a row and their MVP's three singles and a double in 21 trips to the plate certainly didn't help the cause. Still, he's only had 145 plate appearances in the playoffs, so there's time for him to turn it around. But if the Dodgers ever hope to break their now 31-year World Series drought, they're likely going to need him to get hot when it matters in order to do it.

YEAR	TEAM	LVL	AGE	PA	DRC+	VORP	BABIP	BRR	FRAA	WARP
2017	OKL	AAA	21	77	138	8.8	.450	0.8	1B(16): 1.0, CF(2): -0.5	0.6
2017	LAN	MLB	21	548	129	47.9	.299	-0.2	1B(93): 0.7, LF(39): -2.5	2.9
2018	LAN	MLB	22	632	113	39.6	.313	3.3	1B(110): -0.9, CF(78): 2.0	2.8
2019	LAN	MLB	23	661	158	66.2	.302	0.4	RF(115): 13.3, 1B(36): 1.9	8.0
2020	LAN	MLB	24	595	141	47.9	.275	0.5	1B 0, CF 3	5.4

Cody Bellinger, continued

Batted Ball Distribution

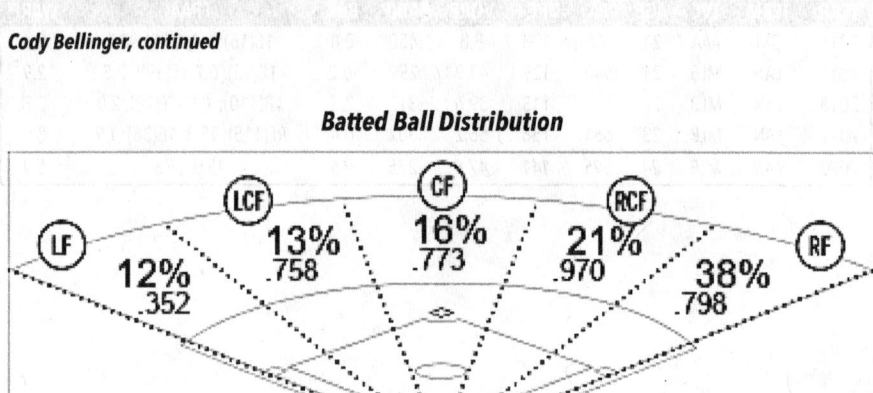

Strike Zone vs LHP   Strike Zone vs RHP

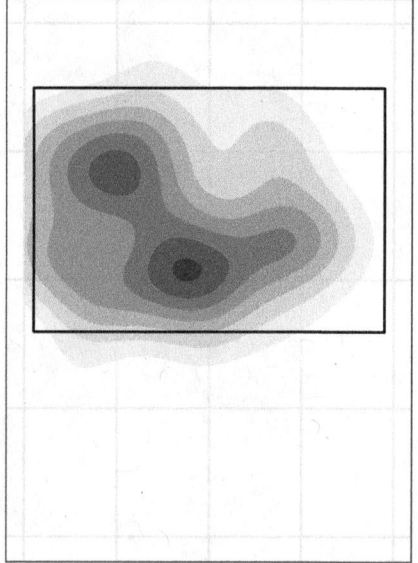

Mookie Betts RF

Born: 10/07/92 Age: 27 Bats: R Throws: R
Height: 5'9" Weight: 180 Origin: Round 5, 2011 Draft (#172 overall)

YEAR	TEAM	LVL	AGE	PA	R	2B	3B	HR	RBI	BB	K	SB	CS	AVG/OBP/SLG
2017	BOS	MLB	24	712	101	46	2	24	102	77	79	26	3	.264/.344/.459
2018	BOS	MLB	25	614	129	47	5	32	80	81	91	30	6	.346/.438/.640
2019	BOS	MLB	26	706	135	40	5	29	80	97	101	16	3	.295/.391/.524
2020	BOS	MLB	27	630	85	38	3	27	91	76	90	22	5	.286/.375/.514

Comparables: Ellis Burks, Chet Lemon, Jim Delsing

What continues to make Betts so special is that he's so damn good at *everything*. He was the game's 16th-best hitter, per DRC+. He was its ninth-best fielder (non-catcher division), per FRAA. He was its sixth-best baserunner, per BRR. And yet, you could call 2019 a down year by his nearly unparalleled standards, as he fell from first in the majors in WARP all the way down to sixth(!) among hitters. That's where we are with Betts; when anyone other than that Mike Trout guy outperforms him, it's a letdown. Now entering his walk year in his age-27 season, Betts is justly poised to threaten the record books with his next contract. He deserves whatever asking price he sets, and if the Red Sox refuse to give it to him, they should be criticized for decades to come. Every franchise only gets a few shots to draft, develop and retain a Hall-of-Fame talent like Betts. Letting one get away is baseball's highest crime, and anyone who tells you otherwise is prioritizing profit margins over fielding the best team possible.

YEAR	TEAM	LVL	AGE	PA	DRC+	VORP	BABIP	BRR	FRAA	WARP
2017	BOS	MLB	24	712	115	31.1	.268	6.2	RF(153): 23.9	5.9
2018	BOS	MLB	25	614	178	76.5	.368	3.8	RF(120): 10.7, CF(14): 0.4	8.9
2019	BOS	MLB	26	706	137	51.7	.309	5.7	RF(132): 11.9, CF(17): 1.6	6.9
2020	BOS	MLB	27	630	134	45.1	.300	3.3	RF 16	6.3

Los Angeles Dodgers 2020

Mookie Betts, continued

Batted Ball Distribution

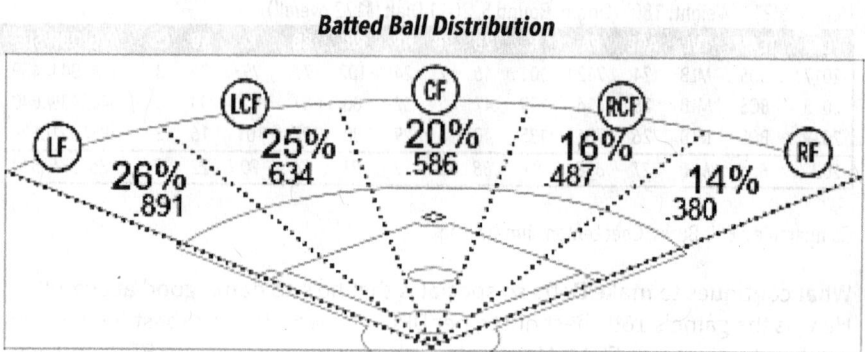

Strike Zone vs LHP   **Strike Zone vs RHP**

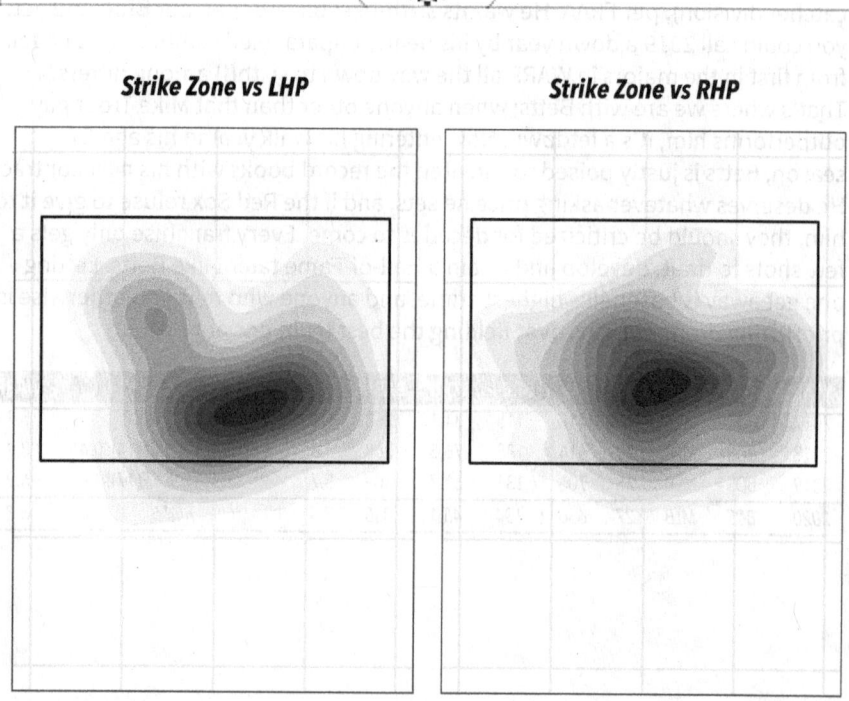

David Freese 1B

Born: 04/28/83   Age: 37   Bats: R   Throws: R
Height: 6'2"   Weight: 213   Origin: Round 9, 2006 Draft (#273 overall)

YEAR	TEAM	LVL	AGE	PA	R	2B	3B	HR	RBI	BB	K	SB	CS	AVG/OBP/SLG
2017	PIT	MLB	34	503	44	16	0	10	52	58	116	0	1	.263/.368/.371
2018	PIT	MLB	35	265	29	10	1	9	42	18	56	0	0	.282/.336/.444
2018	LAN	MLB	35	47	9	2	1	2	9	6	16	0	0	.385/.489/.641
2019	LAN	MLB	36	186	35	13	0	11	29	23	44	0	0	.315/.403/.599
2020	LAN	MLB	37	251	30	11	0	10	33	23	68	1	0	.261/.341/.444

Comparables: Kevin Young, Wes Helms, Kevin Millar

Freese hung up his cleats following the conclusion of the 2019 season. The reliable team dad (Chase Utley) retired, so Freese stepped in as the cool stepdad and was a standout, both in the clubhouse and on the field. While PECOTA pegged him for a .720 OPS, understandably assuming age-related decline, Freese annihilated the ball, outperforming his projection by nearly 300 points of OPS. The only signs of age were the injuries that cost him a couple months of playing time. Even then, he returned down the stretch and continued to add to his postseason legacy by going 4-for-8 with a double in the NLDS. It is remarkable that Freese had so many moments with the Dodgers that eclipsed his 2011 World Series Game 6 heroics with the Cardinals and yet he did, repeatedly.

YEAR	TEAM	LVL	AGE	PA	DRC+	VORP	BABIP	BRR	FRAA	WARP
2017	PIT	MLB	34	503	96	16.8	.336	-4.7	3B(116): 5.3, 1B(3): 0.0	1.6
2018	PIT	MLB	35	265	109	11.6	.330	-0.9	3B(55): 1.7, 1B(15): 1.0	1.3
2018	LAN	MLB	35	47	111	7.1	.619	-0.5	1B(14): -0.4, 3B(3): 0.0	0.0
2019	LAN	MLB	36	186	128	10.3	.374	-0.8	1B(50): -1.6, 3B(2): 0.0	0.8
2020	LAN	MLB	37	251	107	9.4	.332	-1.2	3B 2, 1B 0	1.1

David Freese, continued

Batted Ball Distribution

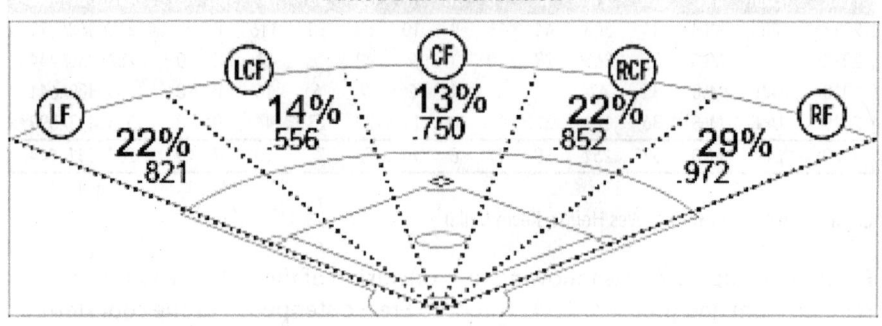

Strike Zone vs LHP

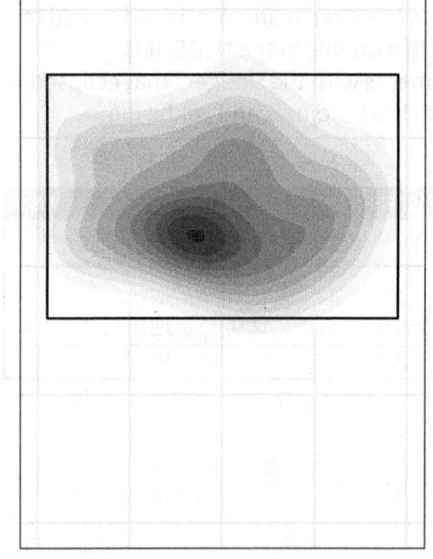

Strike Zone vs RHP

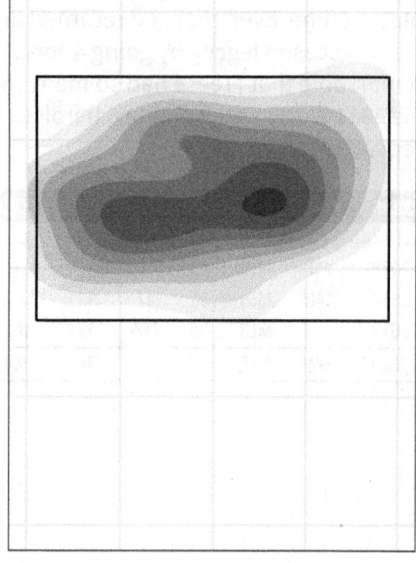

Enrique Hernández UT

Born: 08/24/91   Age: 28   Bats: R   Throws: R
Height: 5'11"   Weight: 192   Origin: Round 6, 2009 Draft (#191 overall)

YEAR	TEAM	LVL	AGE	PA	R	2B	3B	HR	RBI	BB	K	SB	CS	AVG/OBP/SLG
2017	LAN	MLB	25	342	46	24	2	11	37	41	80	3	0	.215/.308/.421
2018	LAN	MLB	26	462	67	17	3	21	52	50	78	3	0	.256/.336/.470
2019	LAN	MLB	27	460	57	19	1	17	64	36	97	4	0	.237/.304/.411
2020	LAN	MLB	28	231	27	9	1	10	31	20	51	1	1	.231/.303/.425

Comparables: Rick Monday, Andrew McCutchen, Mack Jones

This was supposed to be the year Hernández was going to hold down a starting role. He has always been keenly aware of his place on the 25-man hierarchy and has always strived for something more. When the curtains were drawn in 2019, the human meme, the constant jokester, the man who always had something to say … went silent. Or his bat did, anyway. Hernández found himself once again contributing from the edges of the stage rather than the center of it, but contributing all the same. An up-and-down year culminating with some lead-role-worthy performances, notching a major hit in Game 3 of the NLDS and a home run in Game 5. A crowded roster makes it unlikely that he gets another run at a starting role, but Hernández has made clear how valuable he is the top understudy for just about every spot.

YEAR	TEAM	LVL	AGE	PA	DRC+	VORP	BABIP	BRR	FRAA	WARP
2017	LAN	MLB	25	342	89	14.1	.254	2.6	CF(34): 5.8, LF(28): 0.7	1.7
2018	LAN	MLB	26	462	112	29.4	.266	1.9	CF(63): -0.8, 2B(41): -0.3	2.2
2019	LAN	MLB	27	460	91	10.4	.266	1.3	2B(85): 1.1, CF(20): -1.4	1.1
2020	LAN	MLB	28	231	90	5.6	.259	0.6	2B 0, CF 0	0.6

Los Angeles Dodgers 2020

Enrique Hernández, continued

Batted Ball Distribution

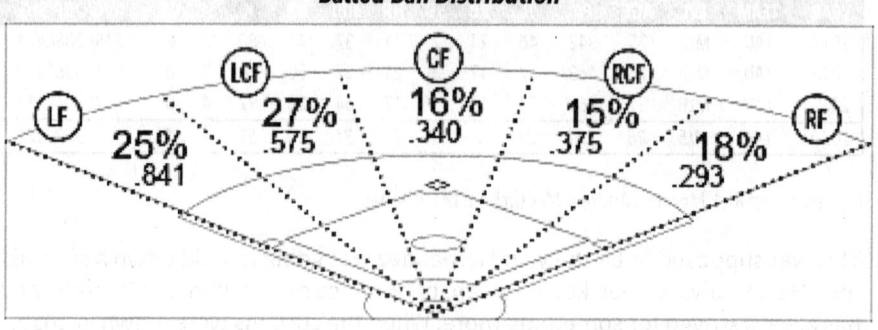

Strike Zone vs LHP   **Strike Zone vs RHP**

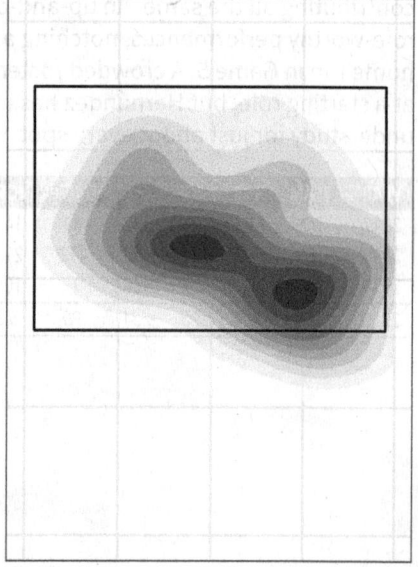

Max Muncy INF

Born: 08/25/90 Age: 29 Bats: L Throws: R
Height: 6'0" Weight: 218 Origin: Round 5, 2012 Draft (#169 overall)

YEAR	TEAM	LVL	AGE	PA	R	2B	3B	HR	RBI	BB	K	SB	CS	AVG/OBP/SLG
2017	OKL	AAA	26	379	62	20	1	12	44	54	84	3	6	.309/.414/.491
2018	OKL	AAA	27	38	7	2	0	2	4	6	5	0	0	.313/.421/.563
2018	LAN	MLB	27	481	75	17	2	35	79	79	131	3	0	.263/.391/.582
2019	LAN	MLB	28	589	101	22	1	35	98	90	149	4	1	.251/.374/.515
2020	LAN	MLB	29	595	85	22	1	34	94	86	159	3	1	.245/.361/.496

Comparables: Matt Tuiasosopo, Ji-Man Choi, Mike Epstein

After coming out of nowhere to get MVP votes in 2018, Muncy wasn't in the mood for a letdown as 2019 marked his first year as an All-Star. His production with the bat (.889 OPS) did take a step back from his ridiculous breakout showing, but he compensated for this by coming into the year in better shape and ended up being a plus defender at three positions (1B/2B/3B). That's all wonderful, but it's even better when paired with Muncy's surprisingly unlimited swag. Between pimping massive dongs with bat drops and telling Madison Bumgarner to go get his homer out of the ocean, Muncy has already cemented himself as a fan favorite. And as one of the key cogs that shows up in the playoffs, hopefully he'll be able to elevate himself to team legend status when all is said and done.

YEAR	TEAM	LVL	AGE	PA	DRC+	VORP	BABIP	BRR	FRAA	WARP
2017	OKL	AAA	26	379	136	35.0	.387	2.0	3B(53): 0.3, 1B(22): 1.9	3.0
2018	OKL	AAA	27	38	127	4.6	.320	0.7	1B(7): 0.1, 3B(3): 0.2	0.3
2018	LAN	MLB	27	481	146	50.2	.299	2.3	1B(84): -0.5, 3B(38): 0.3	3.9
2019	LAN	MLB	28	589	131	40.9	.283	4.1	2B(70): -0.1, 1B(65): 4.2	5.1
2020	LAN	MLB	29	595	125	38.5	.287	2.4	1B 1, 2B -2	3.9

Los Angeles Dodgers 2020

Max Muncy, continued

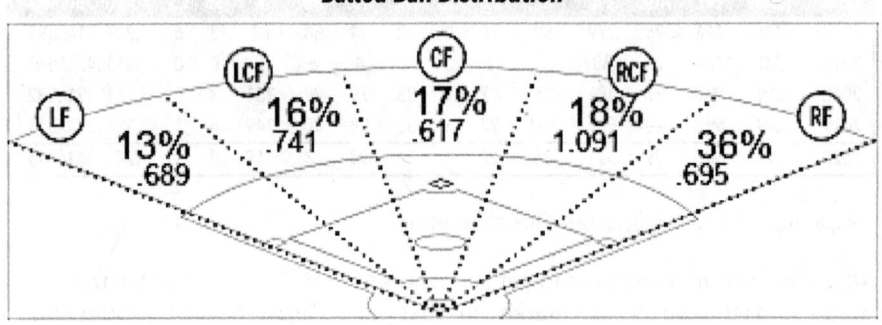

Strike Zone vs LHP   **Strike Zone vs RHP**

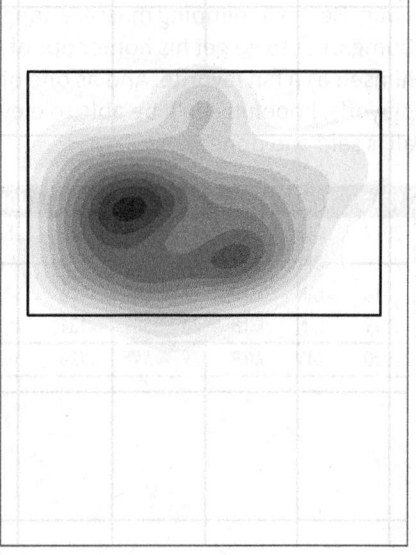

Joc Pederson OF

Born: 04/21/92   Age: 28   Bats: L   Throws: L
Height: 6'1"   Weight: 220   Origin: Round 11, 2010 Draft (#352 overall)

YEAR	TEAM	LVL	AGE	PA	R	2B	3B	HR	RBI	BB	K	SB	CS	AVG/OBP/SLG
2017	OKL	AAA	25	71	8	1	0	3	9	5	14	1	0	.169/.225/.323
2017	LAN	MLB	25	323	44	20	0	11	35	39	68	4	3	.212/.331/.407
2018	LAN	MLB	26	443	65	27	3	25	56	40	85	1	5	.248/.321/.522
2019	LAN	MLB	27	514	83	16	3	36	74	50	111	1	1	.249/.339/.538
2020	LAN	MLB	28	476	69	22	1	30	79	57	110	5	3	.244/.346/.521

Comparables: Harmon Killebrew, Mark McGwire, Kyle Blanks

Pederson was much the same player that he's always been (don't let that OBP bump fool you, it was buoyed by 12 HBPs). What he's always been has been pretty good, too: a strong-side platoon bat that murderizes righties. Pederson benefited from the rabbit ball, turning 11 fewer doubles into 11 more home runs. He's effective at the dish thanks to a violent swing that is the antithesis of the traditional picturesque lefty stroke. It remains aesthetically pleasing though; the visual version of onomatopoeia, where it *looks* like he's hitting the ball as far as it actually ends up flying. He's got one year of team control remaining, and considering the fringe-average to average skill set he provides everywhere other than the plate, it shouldn't surprise to see him on the trade block. The Dodgers emphasis on players with multiple tools generally makes sense as an approach, but they shouldn't overlook the fact that sometimes you just need a sledgehammer.

YEAR	TEAM	LVL	AGE	PA	DRC+	VORP	BABIP	BRR	FRAA	WARP
2017	OKL	AAA	25	71	45	-4.0	.163	-0.2	LF(10): 3.7, CF(4): 0.8	0.1
2017	LAN	MLB	25	323	89	13.8	.241	1.8	CF(92): -9.1, LF(4): -0.4	-0.1
2018	LAN	MLB	26	443	118	26.9	.253	0.9	LF(116): -1.3, CF(32): -2.4	1.9
2019	LAN	MLB	27	514	123	28.3	.249	2.6	LF(84): 0.5, RF(39): 0.0	3.0
2020	LAN	MLB	28	476	124	29.6	.259	2.0	LF -1, RF 0	3.0

Joc Pederson, continued

Batted Ball Distribution

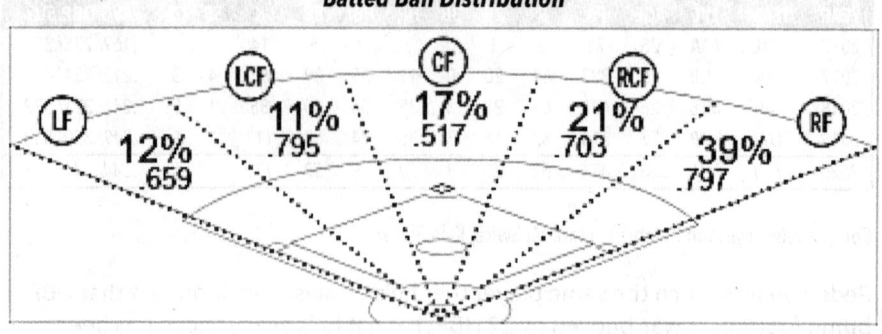

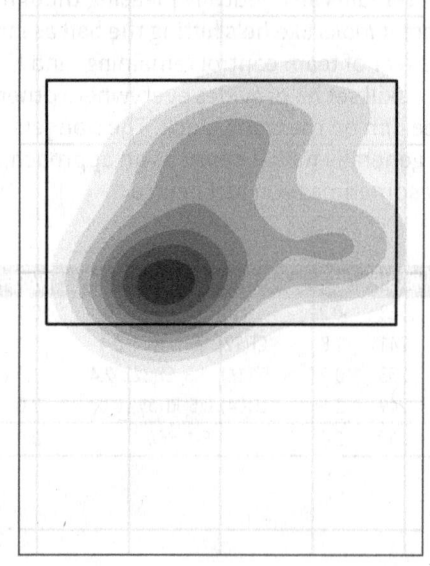
Strike Zone vs LHP

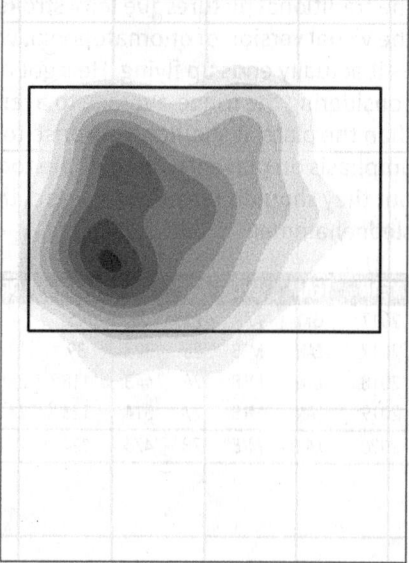
Strike Zone vs RHP

A.J. Pollock CF

Born: 12/05/87   Age: 32   Bats: R   Throws: R
Height: 6'1"   Weight: 212   Origin: Round 1, 2009 Draft (#17 overall)

YEAR	TEAM	LVL	AGE	PA	R	2B	3B	HR	RBI	BB	K	SB	CS	AVG/OBP/SLG
2017	ARI	MLB	29	466	73	33	6	14	49	35	71	20	6	.266/.330/.471
2018	ARI	MLB	30	460	61	21	5	21	65	31	100	13	2	.257/.316/.484
2019	LAN	MLB	31	342	49	15	1	15	47	23	74	5	1	.266/.327/.468
2020	LAN	MLB	32	455	55	21	2	19	62	34	98	17	5	.258/.321/.460

Comparables: Milton Bradley, Fred Lynn, Carlos Gómez

If you squinted at Pollock this past offseason, you might've seen a true center fielder that produced at an All-Star level when healthy, who possessed the tantalizing upside of the down-ballot MVP showing back in 2017. Well, the Dodgers might have been squinting too hard, deciding to give the frequently-injured outfielder four years and a player option for a fifth. That faith was rewarded with the worst season of Pollock's career. It wasn't a surprise to anyone when he missed over two months of the season, but that "produced when healthy" angle went missing, *and* he struggled so much in the field that Cody Bellinger had to take over center field duties. It feels like we've hit rock bottom in this sordid tale, but Pollock came equipped with a diamond-tipped drill of despair. As poorly as the regular season went, Pollock's NLDS performance stands alone: 0-13, one walk, 11 strikeouts and a benching in favor of Matt Beaty. Juan Uribe's transformation from a vitriol-inducing player to a fan favorite lends some optimism for Pollock going forward. At 32, though, it will be an uphill battle to remain healthy and productive, especially as a shift to the corner outfield puts more pressure on his bat. It's unlikely Pollock is as bad going forward as he was in 2019, but only because he'd be hard-pressed to be worse.

YEAR	TEAM	LVL	AGE	PA	DRC+	VORP	BABIP	BRR	FRAA	WARP
2017	ARI	MLB	29	466	100	28.0	.291	0.7	CF(109): 0.3	1.7
2018	ARI	MLB	30	460	106	23.9	.284	1.1	CF(109): -7.6	1.3
2019	LAN	MLB	31	342	98	10.9	.300	-0.3	CF(62): -8.6, LF(18): -0.1	0.2
2020	LAN	MLB	32	455	103	18.3	.294	0.2	CF -5, LF 0	1.3

A.J. Pollock, continued

Batted Ball Distribution

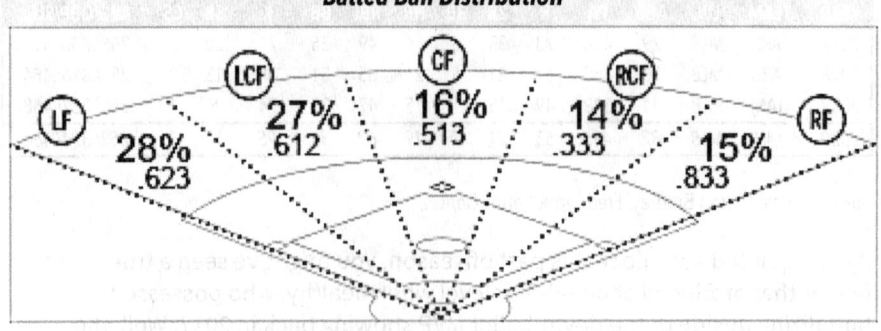

Strike Zone vs LHP

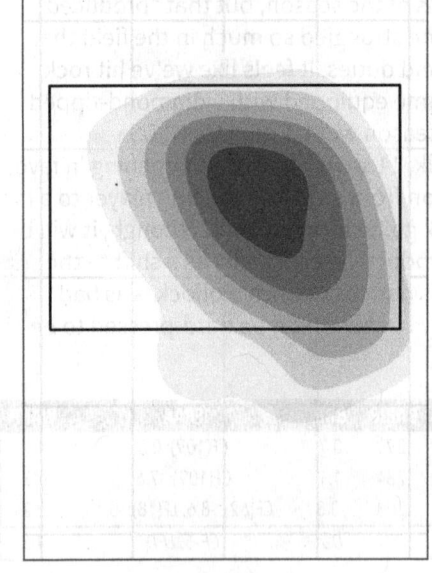

Strike Zone vs RHP

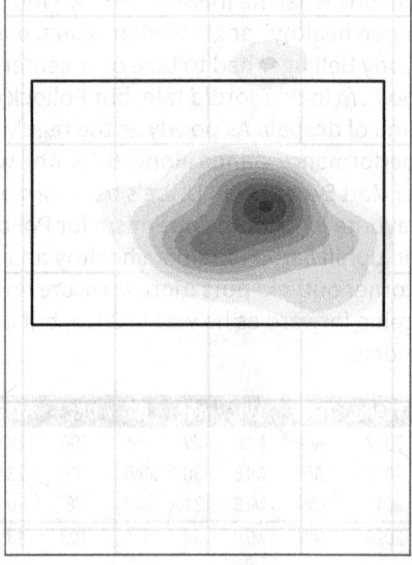

Corey Seager SS

Born: 04/27/94 Age: 26 Bats: L Throws: R
Height: 6'4" Weight: 215 Origin: Round 1, 2012 Draft (#18 overall)

YEAR	TEAM	LVL	AGE	PA	R	2B	3B	HR	RBI	BB	K	SB	CS	AVG/OBP/SLG
2017	LAN	MLB	23	613	85	33	0	22	77	67	131	4	2	.295/.375/.479
2018	LAN	MLB	24	115	13	5	1	2	13	11	17	0	0	.267/.348/.396
2019	LAN	MLB	25	541	82	44	1	19	87	44	98	1	0	.272/.335/.483
2020	LAN	MLB	26	595	70	36	1	24	80	49	117	3	1	.265/.332/.467

Comparables: Carlos Correa, Javier Báez, Cal Ripken Jr.

Seager's first two full seasons with the Dodgers established him as a four-plus win player and perennial All-Star at shortstop, while his third was lost after a mere 26 games thanks to elbow and hip surgeries. Last year brought about some more missed time due to a balky hamstring, and it seemed every time he was getting right at the plate, a muscle would strain or a ligament would tweak. Still, he produced a solid, if not vintage, season and the further removed he is from those major surgeries the better he figures to be. How much he can distance himself from the injury bug remains to be seen, however, and it's possible the 2019 version of Seager is the new normal. Health isn't the only black mark on his ledger either, as a .605 OPS in 31 playoff games hangs over his Dodgers tenure like a dark cloud.

There have been some trade rumblings with Seager's name included, which serves as a convenient representation of his current career crossroads: Is he still a franchise cornerstone or is he just another piece of the puzzle? Seager likely goes nowhere and puts up another quality season, the quality of which will go a long way towards determining his future with the team beyond just the years of team control.

YEAR	TEAM	LVL	AGE	PA	DRC+	VORP	BABIP	BRR	FRAA	WARP
2017	LAN	MLB	23	613	115	57.6	.352	2.2	SS(138): -1.8	4.0
2018	LAN	MLB	24	115	104	7.4	.301	0.8	SS(25): 0.3	0.7
2019	LAN	MLB	25	541	106	30.4	.303	0.7	SS(132): 1.2	3.1
2020	LAN	MLB	26	595	108	30.3	.300	1.4	SS -1	3.1

Corey Seager, continued

Batted Ball Distribution

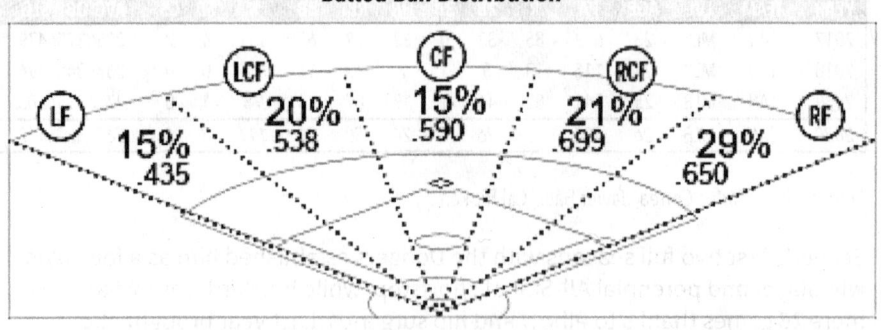

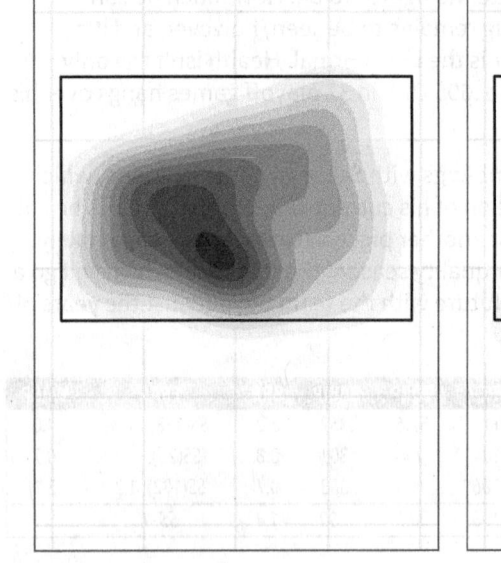

Strike Zone vs LHP

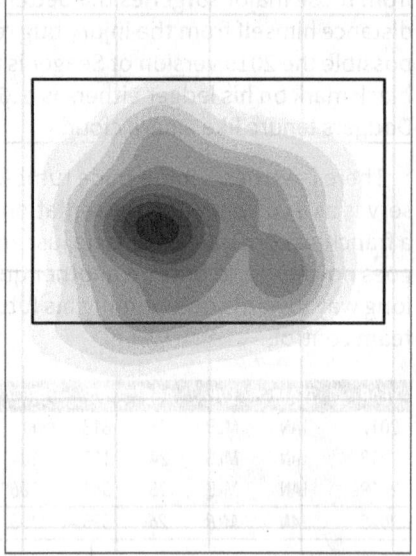

Strike Zone vs RHP

Will Smith C

Born: 03/28/95   Age: 25   Bats: R   Throws: R
Height: 5'10"   Weight: 195   Origin: Round 1, 2016 Draft (#32 overall)

YEAR	TEAM	LVL	AGE	PA	R	2B	3B	HR	RBI	BB	K	SB	CS	AVG/OBP/SLG
2017	RCU	A+	22	305	38	15	3	11	43	37	71	6	2	.232/.355/.448
2018	TUL	AA	23	307	48	14	0	19	53	36	75	4	0	.264/.358/.532
2018	OKL	AAA	23	98	9	4	0	1	6	7	37	1	0	.138/.206/.218
2019	OKL	AAA	24	270	48	11	2	20	54	40	49	1	0	.268/.381/.603
2019	LAN	MLB	24	196	30	9	0	15	42	18	52	2	0	.253/.337/.571
2020	LAN	MLB	25	455	64	19	1	29	75	45	118	2	1	.240/.330/.509

Comparables: Jake Rogers, Gene Tenace, Carlos Santana

YEAR	TEAM	P. COUNT	FRM RUNS	BLK RUNS	THRW RUNS	TOT RUNS
2018	OKL	2087	1.2	0.0	0.0	2.1
2018	TUL	4187	7.0	0.1	0.6	8.4
2019	LAN	6644	2.1	1.2	-0.1	4.1
2019	OKL	7280	0.5	0.0	-1.0	-0.2
2020	LAN	15190	8.3	0.9	-0.3	8.9

The only thing more tired than puns of Will Smith's name is other teams asking for him in trade talks, so rest easy, you won't find any here. You're welcome, everyone. It's hard to believe now, but just four years ago Smith put up a .665 OPS in college with only two homers. Thankfully he took to the Dodgers instruction, adding loft to his swing, and he's never looked back. Smith completed his meteoric rise to prominence in 2019, supplanting both Austin Barnes and Russell Martin to become the starting catcher, and also leaping over fellow top prospect Keibert Ruiz entirely. Of course, there are always concerns with breakout rookie stars, like the 26.5 strikeout rate or posting a .582 OPS in September. But even assuming regression, he looks like an above-average present regular with All-Star potential and that's why the Dodgers are already penciling him in as the 2020 starter.

YEAR	TEAM	LVL	AGE	PA	DRC+	VORP	BABIP	BRR	FRAA	WARP
2017	RCU	A+	22	305	105	16.7	.273	-2.0	C(55): 2.7, 3B(6): -1.0	1.4
2018	TUL	AA	23	307	137	25.5	.295	-1.8	C(33): 7.4, 3B(33): -1.3	2.7
2018	OKL	AAA	23	98	14	-3.8	.216	1.4	C(16): 1.4, 3B(10): 0.3	-0.3
2019	OKL	AAA	24	270	138	30.4	.253	0.9	C(52): -0.1, 3B(1): -0.1	2.5
2019	LAN	MLB	24	196	123	16.0	.264	-0.6	C(46): 4.5	1.9
2020	LAN	MLB	25	455	117	30.0	.265	-0.5	C 10, 3B 0	4.1

Will Smith, continued

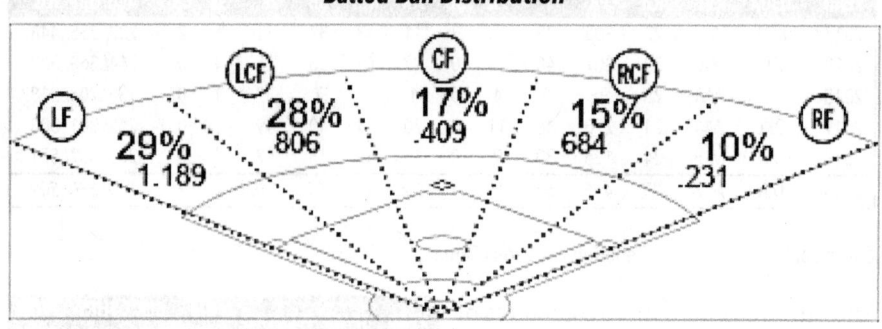

Batted Ball Distribution

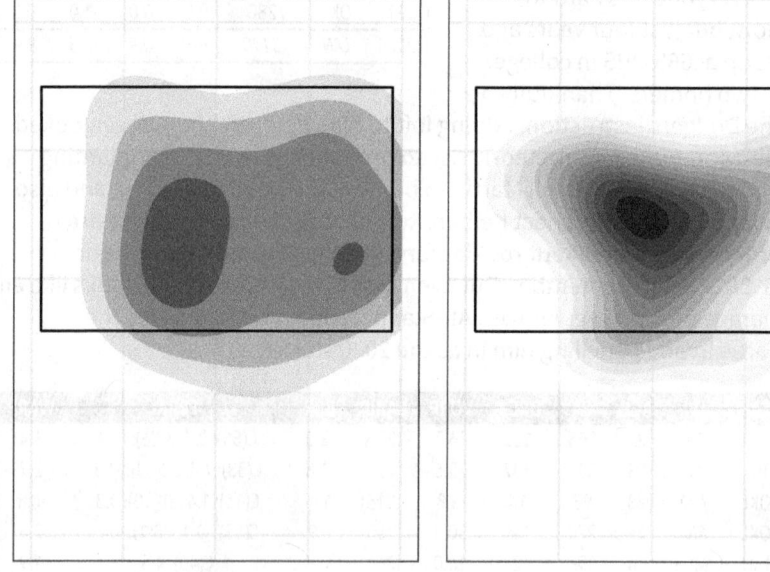

Strike Zone vs LHP   Strike Zone vs RHP

Chris Taylor UT

Born: 08/29/90   Age: 29   Bats: R   Throws: R
Height: 6'1"   Weight: 196   Origin: Round 5, 2012 Draft (#161 overall)

YEAR	TEAM	LVL	AGE	PA	R	2B	3B	HR	RBI	BB	K	SB	CS	AVG/OBP/SLG
2017	OKL	AAA	26	49	8	2	2	1	5	5	5	1	2	.233/.327/.442
2017	LAN	MLB	26	568	85	34	5	21	72	50	142	17	4	.288/.354/.496
2018	LAN	MLB	27	604	85	35	8	17	63	55	178	9	6	.254/.331/.444
2019	LAN	MLB	28	414	52	29	4	12	52	37	115	8	0	.262/.333/.462
2020	LAN	MLB	29	294	32	13	2	9	34	26	84	7	3	.238/.313/.405

Comparables: Roy Smalley, Eugenio Suárez, Brad Miller

Taylor remained productive, if less so, in 2018 despite leading the National League in strikeouts. His propensity for whiffitude didn't engender much love among the fanbase, and an ice-cold April (.171 batting average) led to many suggestions that he go warm up on the face of the sun. Taylor took it all in stride, and proceeded to post a .860 OPS the rest of the way. Pair that with solid defense at six different positions, and you'll find a lot of people pretending they liked him just fine all along. Taylor will get a deserved pay raise this off-season in arbitration and then resume his marauding around the field in a utility role while bringing a quality bat to the plate.

YEAR	TEAM	LVL	AGE	PA	DRC+	VORP	BABIP	BRR	FRAA	WARP
2017	OKL	AAA	26	49	89	2.9	.243	0.6	SS(5): 0.5, CF(3): 0.2	0.3
2017	LAN	MLB	26	568	114	49.7	.361	4.4	CF(49): -2.2, LF(48): 6.6	3.9
2018	LAN	MLB	27	604	103	35.6	.345	0.9	SS(81): 3.7, CF(50): -4.5	2.7
2019	LAN	MLB	28	414	92	11.0	.344	3.0	LF(56): 0.8, SS(39): -4.6	0.8
2020	LAN	MLB	29	294	90	6.1	.317	1.0	SS 0, LF 2	0.8

Chris Taylor, continued

Batted Ball Distribution

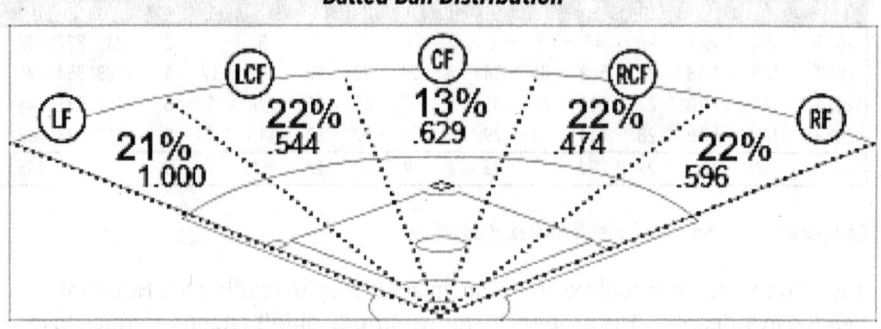

Strike Zone vs LHP **Strike Zone vs RHP**

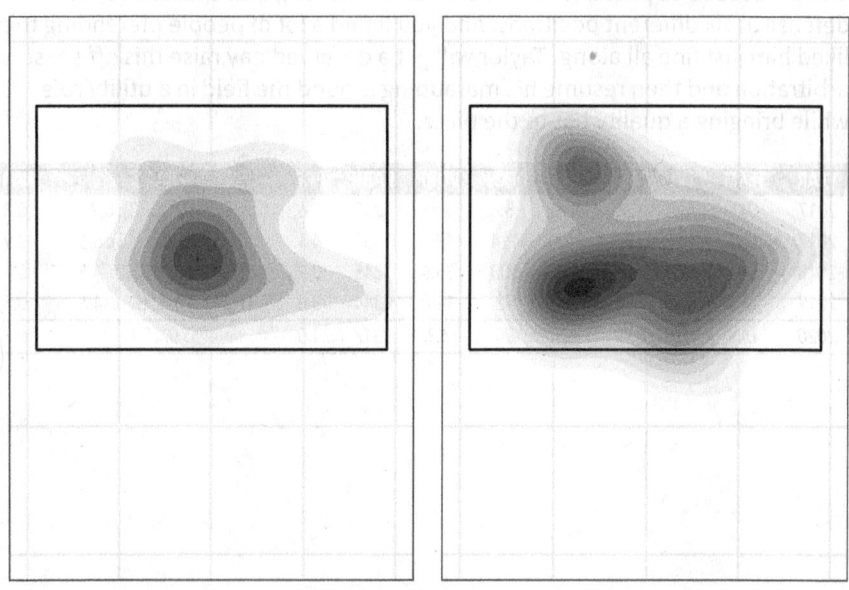

Justin Turner 3B

Born: 11/23/84 Age: 35 Bats: R Throws: R
Height: 5'11" Weight: 202 Origin: Round 7, 2006 Draft (#204 overall)

YEAR	TEAM	LVL	AGE	PA	R	2B	3B	HR	RBI	BB	K	SB	CS	AVG/OBP/SLG
2017	LAN	MLB	32	543	72	32	0	21	71	59	56	7	1	.322/.415/.530
2018	LAN	MLB	33	426	62	31	1	14	52	47	54	2	1	.312/.406/.518
2019	LAN	MLB	34	549	80	24	0	27	67	51	88	2	0	.290/.372/.509
2020	LAN	MLB	35	560	72	27	1	24	79	50	98	5	2	.277/.359/.481

Comparables: Chase Utley, Bill Doran, Bernie Allen

Turner ending his career with the Dodgers without winning a World Series ring would be a travesty. After building himself into an All-Star with the club, JT has been one of the few stars for the team who have performed in the playoffs (.931 OPS). While he may look like a character from a fantasy series, he's not immortal and one has to ask when the breaking point will come. He will be 35 next year and the slow signs of decline are creeping in, especially on defense. Before free agency even officially began, there was already talk about him moving across the diamond to first base. Turner arrived on the team one year into their seven-year run atop the NL West, but he, as much as any player, defines their rise. An early adopter of the swing change that gripped the league, Turner's steady presence and potent bat has driven the Dodgers lineup since he arrived. It would be a shame if his time on the team ends without him hoisting a World Series trophy.

YEAR	TEAM	LVL	AGE	PA	DRC+	VORP	BABIP	BRR	FRAA	WARP
2017	LAN	MLB	32	543	149	62.8	.326	-3.2	3B(121): -5.5	4.4
2018	LAN	MLB	33	426	146	44.3	.334	0.3	3B(96): 11.1	5.1
2019	LAN	MLB	34	549	134	45.2	.304	-1.3	3B(124): 2.2, 2B(1): 0.0	4.5
2020	LAN	MLB	35	560	122	27.9	.302	-1.5	3B 4	3.3

Justin Turner, continued

Batted Ball Distribution

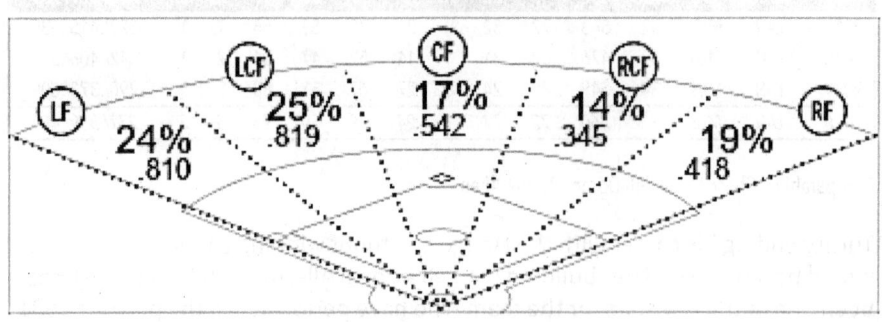

Strike Zone vs LHP **Strike Zone vs RHP**

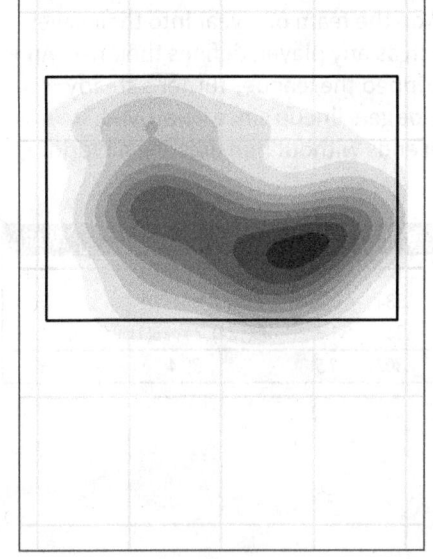
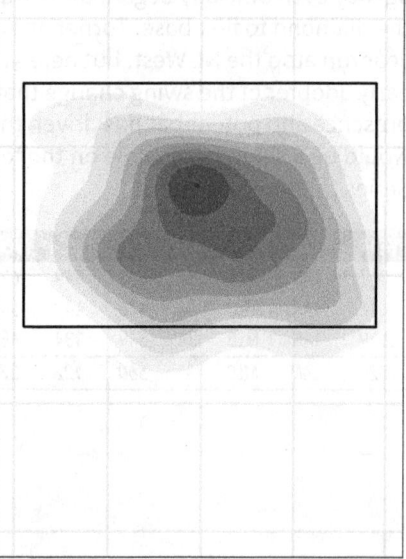

Scott Alexander LHP

Born: 07/10/89 Age: 30 Bats: L Throws: L
Height: 6'2" Weight: 195 Origin: Round 6, 2010 Draft (#179 overall)

YEAR	TEAM	LVL	AGE	W	L	SV	G	GS	IP	H	HR	BB/9	K/9	K	GB%	BABIP
2017	OMA	AAA	27	1	0	0	7	0	7$2^2$	9	1	3.5	4.7	4	78%	.308
2017	KCA	MLB	27	5	4	4	58	0	69	62	3	3.7	7.7	59	73%	.306
2018	LAN	MLB	28	2	1	3	73	1	66	57	4	3.7	7.6	56	72%	.296
2019	LAN	MLB	29	3	2	0	28	0	17^1	17	2	3.6	4.7	9	61%	.263
2020	LAN	MLB	30	2	2	0	37	0	39	38	4	4.0	8.2	36	66%	.300

Comparables: Dan Jennings, Sam Freeman, Kevin Chapman

Hyped as a potential Zack Britton-lite when he was acquired in 2018, Alexander ended up as more like a literally lighter Ray King for the Dodgers. After a rough 2019 in which he couldn't seem to miss any bats, Alexander made his last appearance on June 5 and then started a seemingly endless state of rehab until he suddenly and ominously posted a picture of himself after surgery (for a nerve issue) on September 12. Guess that's one way of announcing your season is over.

YEAR	TEAM	LVL	AGE	WHIP	ERA	DRA	WARP	MPH	FB%	WHF	CSP
2017	OMA	AAA	27	1.57	4.70	4.46	0.1				
2017	KCA	MLB	27	1.30	2.48	4.64	0.4	95.3	93.9	14.3	45.6
2018	LAN	MLB	28	1.27	3.68	5.33	-0.3	95.4	85.6	12.4	46.5
2019	LAN	MLB	29	1.38	3.63	5.52	0.0	94.5	88.9	10.1	44.2
2020	LAN	MLB	30	1.40	4.01	4.26	0.5	94.5	89	12.7	45.1

Los Angeles Dodgers 2020

Scott Alexander, continued

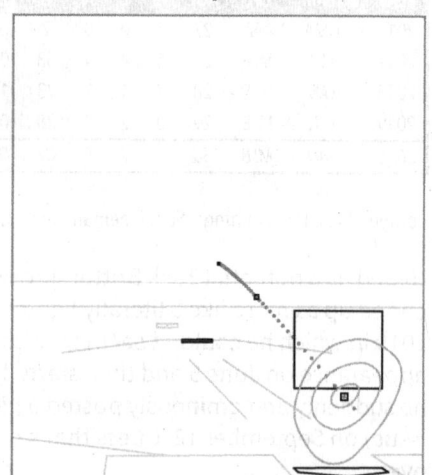

Pitch Shape vs LHH   **Pitch Shape vs RHH**

Type	Frequency	Velocity	H Movement	V Movement
● Fastball				
☐ Sinker	88.5%	93.2 [103]	13 [98]	-23.1 [90]
+ Cutter				
▲ Changeup	3.2%	87.4 [108]	13.2 [91]	-28.8 [96]
✕ Splitter				
▽ Slider	7.9%	84.6 [101]	-2.1 [88]	-36.8 [89]
◇ Curveball				
⊕ Slow Curveball				
✱ Knuckleball				
▼ Screwball				

Walker Buehler RHP

Born: 07/28/94 Age: 25 Bats: R Throws: R
Height: 6'2" Weight: 185 Origin: Round 1, 2015 Draft (#24 overall)

YEAR	TEAM	LVL	AGE	W	L	SV	G	GS	IP	H	HR	BB/9	K/9	K	GB%	BABIP
2017	RCU	A+	22	0	0	0	5	5	16¹	8	0	2.8	14.9	27	57%	.267
2017	TUL	AA	22	2	2	0	11	11	49	40	5	2.8	11.8	64	52%	.315
2017	OKL	AAA	22	1	1	1	12	3	23¹	19	1	4.2	13.1	34	62%	.333
2017	LAN	MLB	22	1	0	0	8	0	9¹	11	2	7.7	11.6	12	67%	.409
2018	OKL	AAA	23	1	0	0	3	3	13	10	0	2.8	11.1	16	61%	.303
2018	LAN	MLB	23	8	5	0	24	23	137¹	95	12	2.4	9.9	151	50%	.248
2019	LAN	MLB	24	14	4	0	30	30	182¹	153	20	1.8	10.6	215	43%	.290
2020	LAN	MLB	25	13	8	0	29	29	178	155	23	2.6	10.6	210	44%	.298

Comparables: Matt Harvey, Rafael Montero, Max Scherzer

It says a lot about Buehler's talent that not being in the top five for NL Cy Young Award voting this year was surprising, but that's just how far expectations have risen for the 25-year-old. In his defense, Buehler was a top-five level pitcher for much of the season after starting slowly in April (5.22 ERA) following missing most of spring training due to not feeling right. Following the ominous start to the year, he settled down beginning in May, and turned in a 2.88 ERA the rest of the season.

Despite his age, Buehler has already taken the torch from Clayton Kershaw as the Dodgers ace and is running with it. It was Buehler who the Dodgers have trusted in big games of late, and aside from his playoff debut he's repaid their trust with excellent results. Ending 31 years of futility is a lot of pressure to heap on Buehler's wiry frame, but the 2020 hopes of the Dodgers will in large part rest on his shoulders and his expected ascent to perennial Cy Young Award candidate.

YEAR	TEAM	LVL	AGE	WHIP	ERA	DRA	WARP	MPH	FB%	WHF	CSP
2017	RCU	A+	22	0.80	1.10	1.53	0.7				
2017	TUL	AA	22	1.12	3.49	3.22	1.1				
2017	OKL	AAA	22	1.29	4.63	1.43	1.0				
2017	LAN	MLB	22	2.04	7.71	4.10	0.1	99.8	69.8	11.5	47.9
2018	OKL	AAA	23	1.08	2.08	2.21	0.5				
2018	LAN	MLB	23	0.96	2.62	3.21	3.3	98.5	59.6	12.6	49.5
2019	LAN	MLB	24	1.04	3.26	2.89	5.7	98.5	60.2	13.4	49.8
2020	LAN	MLB	25	1.16	3.08	3.47	4.6	98.2	61.6	13.4	50.4

Los Angeles Dodgers 2020

Walker Buehler, continued

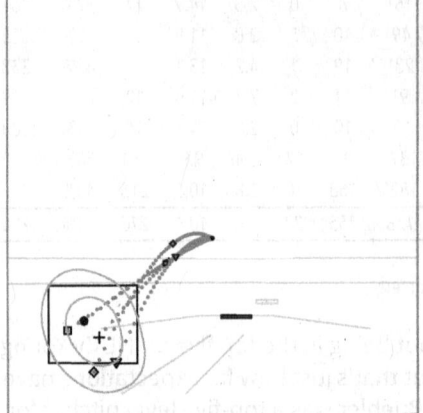

Pitch Shape vs LHH

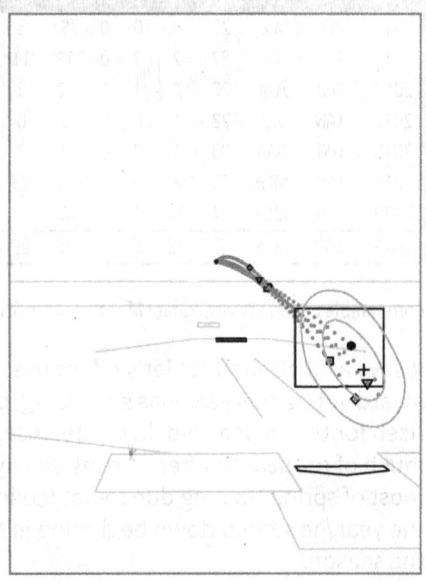

Pitch Shape vs RHH

Type	Frequency	Velocity	H Movement	V Movement
● Fastball	53.2%	96.8 [113]	-3.9 [113]	-10.4 [115]
☐ Sinker	7.0%	96.8 [122]	-11.5 [107]	-14.3 [121]
+ Cutter	13.6%	92.9 [126]	5.2 [120]	-20 [115]
▲ Changeup				
✕ Splitter				
▽ Slider	13.6%	87 [111]	10.1 [121]	-33.1 [100]
◇ Curveball	12.2%	81 [108]	9.7 [109]	-51.9 [91]
✦ Slow Curveball				
✱ Knuckleball				
▼ Screwball				

Caleb Ferguson LHP

Born: 07/02/96 Age: 23 Bats: R Throws: L
Height: 6'3" Weight: 226 Origin: Round 38, 2014 Draft (#1149 overall)

YEAR	TEAM	LVL	AGE	W	L	SV	G	GS	IP	H	HR	BB/9	K/9	K	GB%	BABIP
2017	RCU	A+	20	9	4	0	25	24	122^1	113	6	4.0	10.3	140	46%	.335
2018	TUL	AA	21	3	0	0	8	8	39	31	2	2.3	9.2	40	42%	.284
2018	OKL	AAA	21	0	0	0	2	2	8	6	0	7.9	13.5	12	21%	.316
2018	LAN	MLB	21	7	2	2	29	3	49	43	8	2.2	10.8	59	47%	.292
2019	OKL	AAA	22	0	0	1	13	1	15^1	9	1	2.9	15.8	27	50%	.333
2019	LAN	MLB	22	1	2	0	46	2	44^2	39	7	5.4	10.9	54	40%	.291
2020	LAN	MLB	23	2	2	0	32	0	34	31	5	3.8	9.5	36	41%	.286

Comparables: Jack Flaherty, Michael Kirkman, Logan Allen

After emerging as a viable starting pitching prospect, Ferguson was moved to the 'pen for the Dodgers last year and excelled in the role. While the Dodgers claimed they still wanted to develop him as a starter, he eventually returned to relief and his future seemed primed to be at the back-end of a bullpen. A strong initial performance didn't augur a repeat performance, however. Through mid-August, Ferguson was a disaster, posting a 6.04 ERA. Thanks to an adjustment pitching coach Rick Honeycutt made to his curve grip, Ferguson seemed to regain his old form down the stretch, finishing with a 2.76 ERA over his final 16 1/3 innings. With the relief corps still a question mark going into 2020, the Dodgers will need Ferguson to replicate his late-season form over a whole year.

YEAR	TEAM	LVL	AGE	WHIP	ERA	DRA	WARP	MPH	FB%	WHF	CSP
2017	RCU	A+	20	1.37	2.87	3.90	1.9				
2018	TUL	AA	21	1.05	1.38	2.73	1.2				
2018	OKL	AAA	21	1.62	2.25	4.02	0.1				
2018	LAN	MLB	21	1.12	3.49	3.17	1.0	96.3	71.9	12.5	54.7
2019	OKL	AAA	22	0.91	1.76	1.28	0.7				
2019	LAN	MLB	22	1.48	4.84	4.92	0.2	96.4	78	11.3	49.3
2020	LAN	MLB	23	1.34	4.11	4.35	0.4	96.3	78	12.3	53.5

Los Angeles Dodgers 2020

Caleb Ferguson, continued

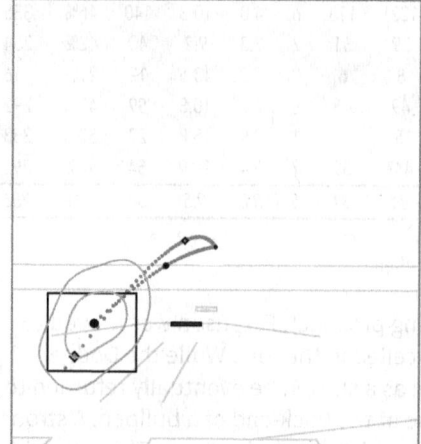
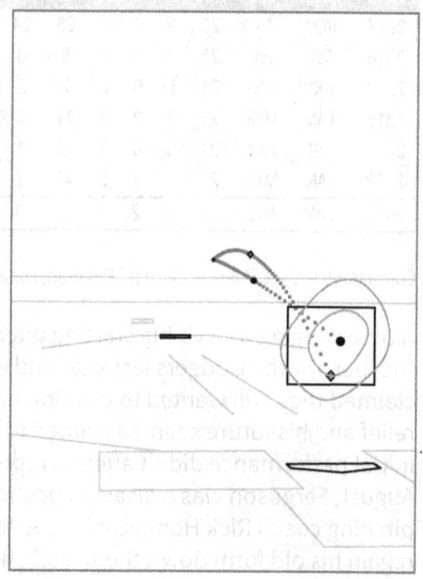

Type	Frequency	Velocity	H Movement	V Movement
● Fastball	78.0%	94.7 [107]	9.1 [90]	-12.6 [109]
☐ Sinker				
+ Cutter				
▲ Changeup				
✕ Splitter				
▽ Slider				
◇ Curveball	21.8%	76.4 [93]	-10 [110]	-57 [80]
✦ Slow Curveball				
✱ Knuckleball				
▼ Screwball				

Dylan Floro RHP

Born: 12/27/90 Age: 29 Bats: L Throws: R
Height: 6'2" Weight: 203 Origin: Round 13, 2012 Draft (#422 overall)

YEAR	TEAM	LVL	AGE	W	L	SV	G	GS	IP	H	HR	BB/9	K/9	K	GB%	BABIP
2017	IOW	AAA	26	3	2	1	25	2	48^2	54	9	1.5	4.8	26	63%	.274
2017	OKL	AAA	26	0	1	1	8	0	11^1	18	0	2.4	9.5	12	58%	.474
2017	CHN	MLB	26	0	0	0	3	0	9^2	15	2	1.9	5.6	6	53%	.382
2018	CIN	MLB	27	3	2	0	25	0	36^1	39	2	3.0	6.7	27	57%	.314
2018	LAN	MLB	27	3	1	0	29	0	27^2	18	1	3.6	10.1	31	55%	.250
2019	LAN	MLB	28	5	3	0	50	0	46^2	46	4	2.7	8.1	42	52%	.302
2020	LAN	MLB	29	2	2	0	32	0	34	33	4	2.4	8.3	31	53%	.300

Comparables: Chasen Bradford, Matt Bowman, Shane Carle

Floro was a revelation after coming over in a trade from the Reds in 2018, using his hard sinker to miss a surprising amount of at-bats while performing like a quality back-end relief arm. However, he struggled to repeat his success in 2019, ending the year with an ERA over 4.00 and missing out on the playoff roster. Whether his year was typical reliever variation or evidence of why he's been with four teams in four years will be an important factor in determining whether he's a solid middle relief option going forward.

YEAR	TEAM	LVL	AGE	WHIP	ERA	DRA	WARP	MPH	FB%	WHF	CSP
2017	IOW	AAA	26	1.27	3.88	4.89	0.2				
2017	OKL	AAA	26	1.85	5.56	5.67	0.0				
2017	CHN	MLB	26	1.76	6.52	6.19	-0.1	93.5	67.7	9.8	54.8
2018	CIN	MLB	27	1.40	2.72	5.25	-0.1	95.3	62.4	9.8	48.1
2018	LAN	MLB	27	1.05	1.63	3.14	0.6	95.8	64.8	15.3	45
2019	LAN	MLB	28	1.29	4.24	4.56	0.4	95.6	67.5	13.4	50.9
2020	LAN	MLB	29	1.26	3.65	4.01	0.5	94.8	65.5	12.6	50.5

Dylan Floro, continued

Pitch Shape vs LHH

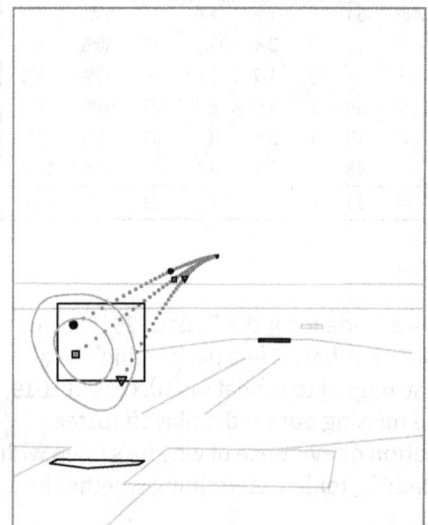

Pitch Shape vs RHH

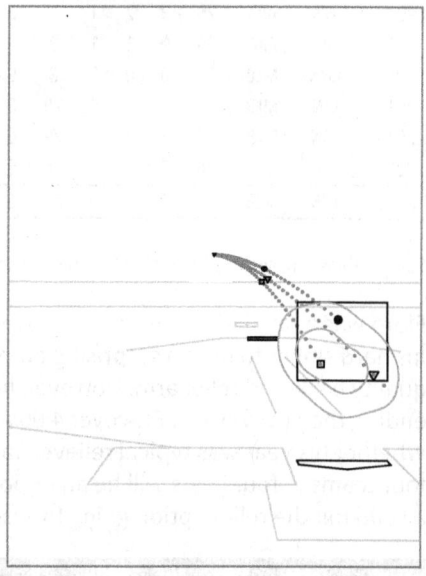

Type	Frequency	Velocity	H Movement	V Movement
● Fastball	19.3%	94.4 [106]	-8.3 [94]	-14 [105]
☐ Sinker	48.1%	93.9 [107]	-13.7 [93]	-18.8 [105]
+ Cutter				
▲ Changeup	3.8%	87.4 [108]	-14.2 [86]	-26.3 [103]
✕ Splitter				
▽ Slider	28.5%	88.1 [116]	1.9 [87]	-26.1 [120]
◇ Curveball				
◈ Slow Curveball				
✱ Knuckleball				
▼ Screwball				

Tony Gonsolin   RHP

Born: 05/14/94   Age: 26   Bats: R   Throws: R
Height: 6'3"   Weight: 205   Origin: Round 9, 2016 Draft (#281 overall)

YEAR	TEAM	LVL	AGE	W	L	SV	G	GS	IP	H	HR	BB/9	K/9	K	GB%	BABIP
2017	GRL	A	23	0	1	1	3	0	8	8	2	0.0	13.5	12	38%	.316
2017	RCU	A+	23	7	5	5	39	0	62	61	5	2.6	10.6	73	43%	.344
2018	RCU	A+	24	4	2	0	17	17	83²	72	5	2.8	11.4	106	38%	.319
2018	TUL	AA	24	6	0	0	9	9	44¹	32	3	3.2	9.9	49	39%	.261
2019	OKL	AAA	25	2	4	0	13	13	41¹	41	4	4.6	10.9	50	37%	.327
2019	LAN	MLB	25	4	2	1	11	6	40	26	4	3.4	8.3	37	43%	.208
2020	LAN	MLB	26	6	5	0	30	15	90	79	13	3.7	8.7	86	39%	.275

Comparables: John Curtiss, Brock Stewart, Trevor Richards

The guy best known for breaking out the cat meme shirts during spring training earned notoriety for a lot more than that. Gonsolin broke out, himself, in 2018, running amok in Tulsa. He opened 2019 at Triple-A before making his big-league debut, throwing 40 innings of sub-3.00 ERA ball split between starting and relieving. With a fastball sitting in the 92-95 mph range, Gonsolin effectively uses a four-pitch mix, and even if things don't work out in the rotation, his fastball and split combo should find a place in the 'pen. The long-locked righty was on the outside looking in when it came to the playoff roster, but figures to factor in heavily as the Dodgers once again rely on their depth heading into 2020.

YEAR	TEAM	LVL	AGE	WHIP	ERA	DRA	WARP	MPH	FB%	WHF	CSP
2017	GRL	A	23	1.00	3.38	3.29	0.2				
2017	RCU	A+	23	1.27	3.92	3.30	1.2				
2018	RCU	A+	24	1.17	2.69	2.72	2.5				
2018	TUL	AA	24	1.08	2.44	3.00	1.2				
2019	OKL	AAA	25	1.50	4.35	2.98	1.5				
2019	LAN	MLB	25	1.02	2.92	4.19	0.6	95.4	48.3	12.5	43.1
2020	LAN	MLB	26	1.29	3.72	4.04	1.7	95.0	49.2	12.8	43.9

Los Angeles Dodgers 2020

Tony Gonsolin, continued

Pitch Shape vs LHH

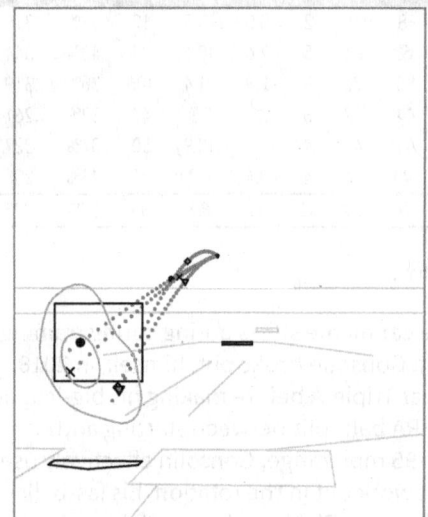

Pitch Shape vs RHH

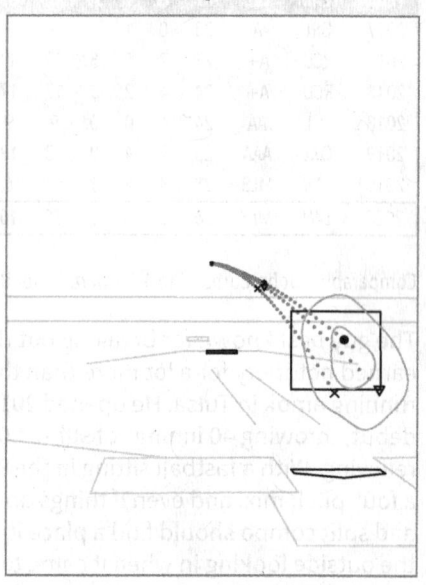

Type	Frequency	Velocity	H Movement	V Movement
● Fastball	48.3%	93.6 [103]	-6.2 [103]	-12.3 [109]
☐ Sinker				
+ Cutter				
▲ Changeup				
✕ Splitter	24.7%	86.5 [106]	-11.5 [87]	-22 [124]
▽ Slider	16.9%	88 [115]	2.4 [89]	-25.7 [121]
◇ Curveball	10.1%	80.5 [106]	3.4 [84]	-50.9 [93]
◈ Slow Curveball				
✳ Knuckleball				
▼ Screwball				

Brusdar Graterol RHP

Born: 08/26/98 Age: 21 Bats: R Throws: R
Height: 6'1" Weight: 265 Origin: International Free Agent, 2014

YEAR	TEAM	LVL	AGE	W	L	SV	G	GS	IP	H	HR	BB/9	K/9	K	GB%	BABIP
2017	TWI	RK	18	2	0	0	5	2	19^1	10	1	1.9	9.8	21	58%	.205
2017	ELZ	RK	18	2	1	0	5	5	20^2	16	1	3.9	10.5	24	59%	.300
2018	CDR	A	19	3	2	0	8	8	41^1	30	3	2.0	11.1	51	64%	.270
2018	FTM	A+	19	5	2	0	11	11	60^2	59	0	2.8	8.3	56	49%	.343
2019	PEN	AA	20	6	0	1	12	9	52^2	32	2	3.6	8.5	50	56%	.233
2019	MIN	MLB	20	1	1	0	10	0	9^2	10	1	1.9	9.3	10	52%	.346
2020	MIN	MLB	21	4	3	0	30	8	64	65	8	3.3	7.9	56	53%	.305

Comparables: Chris Tillman, Lucas Giolito, Jenrry Mejia

Graterol presents a proposition as old as baseball time: big boy, big stuff, big question marks about health and durability. Major-league hitters received a preview of coming attractions late last season, when he debuted and introduced his triple-digit heat. It's an elite two-way offering, with gnarly two-seam sink or four-seam ride, and it looked more than capable of paving the way. The way he loads his shoulder proved problematic, however, and he missed a chunk of the season with an impingement—a concerning development for a guy with a catastrophic arm injury already headlining his medical records. There's enough projection to his secondaries that he should force his way firmly into the team's short-term rotation plans, and there's also more than enough short-burst velocity to fall back on.

YEAR	TEAM	LVL	AGE	WHIP	ERA	DRA	WARP	MPH	FB%	WHF	CSP
2017	TWI	RK	18	0.72	1.40	1.12	1.0				
2017	ELZ	RK	18	1.21	3.92	2.38	0.8				
2018	CDR	A	19	0.94	2.18	2.45	1.4				
2018	FTM	A+	19	1.29	3.12	4.61	0.5				
2019	PEN	AA	20	1.01	1.71	2.93	1.3				
2019	MIN	MLB	20	1.24	4.66	3.44	0.2	100.4	67.4	9.7	53.1
2020	MIN	MLB	21	1.39	4.62	4.58	0.6	100.6	70.6	10.2	55.6

Los Angeles Dodgers 2020

Brusdar Graterol, continued

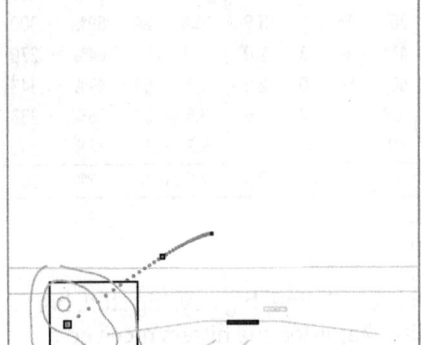
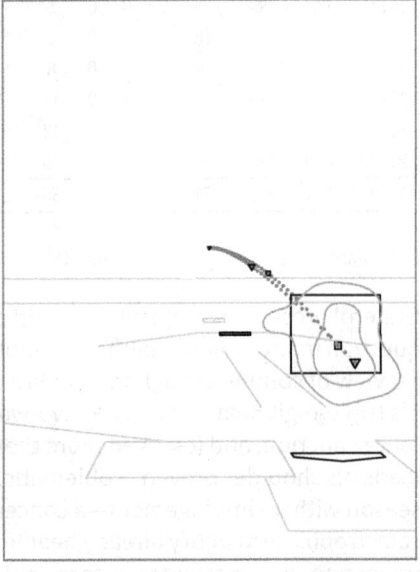

Type	Frequency	Velocity	H Movement	V Movement
● Fastball	11.8%	98.8 [118]	-7.1 [99]	-13.9 [105]
☐ Sinker	55.6%	99 [133]	-11.8 [105]	-18.5 [107]
+ Cutter				
▲ Changeup				
✕ Splitter				
▽ Slider	30.6%	88.2 [116]	7.6 [111]	-27.1 [117]
◇ Curveball				
✦ Slow Curveball				
✱ Knuckleball				
▼ Screwball				

Kenley Jansen RHP

Born: 09/30/87 Age: 32 Bats: B Throws: R
Height: 6'5" Weight: 265 Origin: International Free Agent, 2004

YEAR	TEAM	LVL	AGE	W	L	SV	G	GS	IP	H	HR	BB/9	K/9	K	GB%	BABIP
2017	LAN	MLB	29	5	0	41	65	0	68¹	44	5	0.9	14.4	109	40%	.291
2018	LAN	MLB	30	1	5	38	69	0	71²	54	13	2.1	10.3	82	36%	.234
2019	LAN	MLB	31	5	3	33	62	0	63	51	9	2.3	11.4	80	36%	.273
2020	LAN	MLB	32	3	2	41	53	0	56	42	9	2.4	11.1	69	35%	.257

Comparables: Craig Kimbrel, Francisco Rodríguez, David Robertson

Jansen has had a remarkable career, starting off with a ridiculous eight-year run from his debut in 2010 to 2017. He was effectively the best reliever in baseball over that stretch, posting a 2.08 ERA in 477 innings and striking out an unreal 741 against just 126 walks. Unfortunately, all good things must come to an end, and in the past two seasons, his mortality has been laid bare as his strikeouts have dipped and his walks ticked up. Kenley ended 2019 with a career-high 3.71 ERA, almost a full run higher than any other year in his career. Perhaps no other stat illustrates his newfound hittability better than having surrendered 35 homers over his first eight years and 22 homers in his last two. A lot of ink has been spilled on trying to figure out what's wrong with Jansen and how to get him back to his old form, but he's now 32 and it seems fairly obvious that turning back the clock is unlikely. Still, the Dodgers need him to find a way—whether it be increased use of his slider and/or two-seamer—to become a viable first-division closer again because their 'pen doesn't work without one. As it is, 1988 continues to drift further into the rear-view mirror.

YEAR	TEAM	LVL	AGE	WHIP	ERA	DRA	WARP	MPH	FB%	WHF	CSP
2017	LAN	MLB	29	0.75	1.32	1.90	2.5	96.0	92	19.8	51.8
2018	LAN	MLB	30	0.99	3.01	2.56	2.0	95.2	94.2	14.6	49
2019	LAN	MLB	31	1.06	3.71	3.51	1.3	94.4	87.7	17.2	47.7
2020	LAN	MLB	32	1.01	2.54	3.03	1.5	94.1	90.2	16.7	48.7

Kenley Jansen, continued

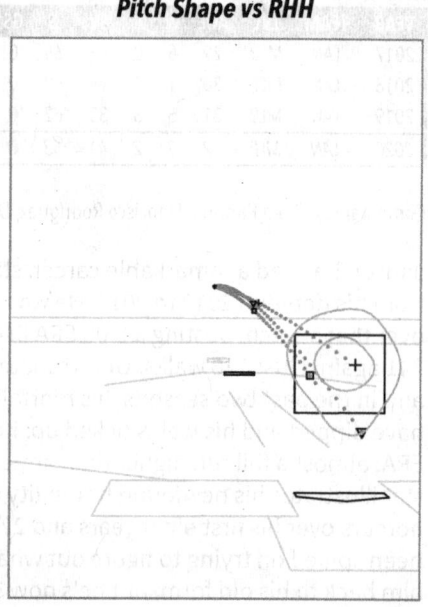

Type	Frequency	Velocity	H Movement	V Movement
● Fastball				
☐ Sinker	13.5%	93.5 [105]	-7.3 [135]	-12.3 [128]
+ Cutter	74.2%	92.1 [121]	6.9 [130]	-15.5 [132]
▲ Changeup				
✕ Splitter				
▽ Slider	12.3%	82 [90]	6.3 [106]	-39.5 [81]
◇ Curveball				
⊕ Slow Curveball				
✽ Knuckleball				
▼ Screwball				

Joe Kelly RHP

Born: 06/09/88   Age: 32   Bats: R   Throws: R
Height: 6'1"   Weight: 174   Origin: Round 3, 2009 Draft (#98 overall)

YEAR	TEAM	LVL	AGE	W	L	SV	G	GS	IP	H	HR	BB/9	K/9	K	GB%	BABIP
2017	BOS	MLB	29	4	1	0	54	0	58	42	3	4.2	8.1	52	51%	.252
2018	BOS	MLB	30	4	2	2	73	0	65^2	57	4	4.4	9.3	68	49%	.301
2019	LAN	MLB	31	5	4	1	55	0	51^1	49	6	3.9	10.9	62	63%	.323
2020	LAN	MLB	32	2	2	4	48	0	50	48	6	3.9	9.7	54	56%	.312

Comparables: Jeff Manship, Chad Bettis, Anthony Bass

Can someone help us off this ride? Sure, yes, "Joe Kelly has great stuff" is a meme built around his inconsistency of results despite his ability, but nothing could've prepared us for his 2019. He began his Dodgers career by attempting to become the most hated member of the team, giving up a 10.13 ERA in around a month and was responsible for ~25 percent of the team's losses to that point. Then something clicked and Kelly started pitching like an elite setup man, putting up a 1.69 ERA over a four-month stretch in the middle of the season. Just when it seemed like he would be the answer to the Dodgers bullpen problems, he surrendered a 7.50 ERA in about the final month. Worse yet he pitched just once after mid-September due to vague soreness that still hasn't been explained. But wait! There's more! Kelly then gave up six runs in 2 1/3 innings in the NLDS, including surrendering the series-losing grand slam in Game 5. All in all, he was a replacement-level relief option, which isn't an ideal outcome from the team's big free agent addition. The hope going forward is that Kelly will be more like he was the middle of last year and not like the bookends, but at this point hope is all it is. At least he has great stuff.

YEAR	TEAM	LVL	AGE	WHIP	ERA	DRA	WARP	MPH	FB%	WHF	CSP
2017	BOS	MLB	29	1.19	2.79	4.00	0.8	101.4	64.3	11.6	45.2
2018	BOS	MLB	30	1.36	4.39	4.56	0.3	100.4	55.4	11.4	45.8
2019	LAN	MLB	31	1.38	4.56	3.27	1.2	99.7	50.9	11.1	48.4
2020	LAN	MLB	32	1.39	4.05	4.27	0.6	99.4	55.5	11.2	46.3

Joe Kelly, continued

Pitch Shape vs LHH

Pitch Shape vs RHH

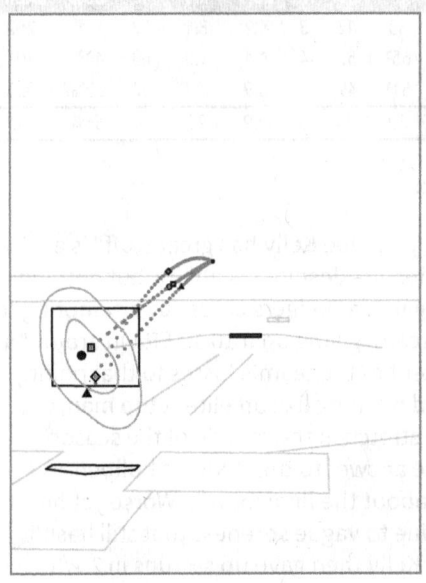

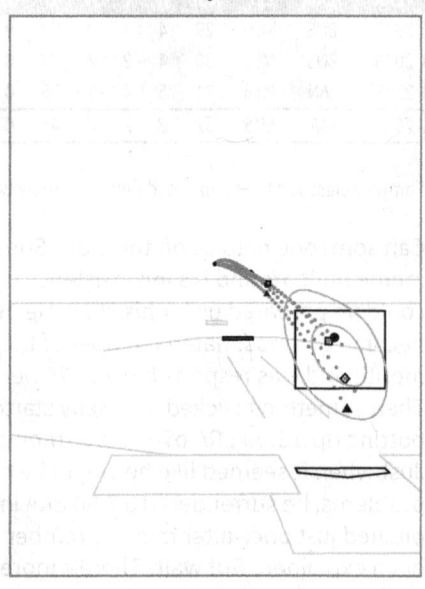

Type		Frequency	Velocity	H Movement	V Movement
●	Fastball	28.1%	97.9 [116]	-7.9 [95]	-13 [108]
□	Sinker	22.7%	98.5 [131]	-13.2 [96]	-16.6 [113]
+	Cutter				
▲	Changeup	12.6%	88 [110]	-14.4 [85]	-25.8 [105]
×	Splitter				
▽	Slider				
◇	Curveball	36.5%	87.4 [129]	9.6 [109]	-43.3 [109]
⊕	Slow Curveball				
✳	Knuckleball				
▼	Screwball				

Clayton Kershaw LHP

Born: 03/19/88   Age: 32   Bats: L   Throws: L
Height: 6'4"   Weight: 226   Origin: Round 1, 2006 Draft (#7 overall)

YEAR	TEAM	LVL	AGE	W	L	SV	G	GS	IP	H	HR	BB/9	K/9	K	GB%	BABIP
2017	LAN	MLB	29	18	4	0	27	27	175	136	23	1.5	10.4	202	49%	.267
2018	LAN	MLB	30	9	5	0	26	26	161[1]	139	17	1.6	8.6	155	50%	.274
2019	LAN	MLB	31	16	5	0	29	28	178[1]	145	28	2.1	9.5	189	49%	.264
2020	LAN	MLB	32	13	7	0	28	28	171	143	24	2.1	9.7	183	49%	.273

Comparables: Sid Fernandez, Madison Bumgarner, Stephen Strasburg

Kershaw seems to be stuck in his own personal "Groundhog Day" except over the course of a baseball season. While he's no longer invincible during the regular season, he's still continued to prove that betting against him finding a way to be effective is for fools. His 2019 ERA was his highest since 2008 and he surrendered 28 homers. He once again managed to stave off any *precipitous* decline despite his fastball now sitting around 90 mph and his slider struggling to find separation. Tragically, like in past years, Kershaw's postseason was worse than expected. He lost a close Game 2 and then was pushed into the decisive Game 5 by Dave Roberts, blowing a two-run lead in the seventh inning on back-to-back pitches via the home-run ball, once again reliving his October nightmare.

In the aftermath, Kershaw seemed a bit broken by it, admitting that the playoff talk surrounding him was less a narrative and more a truth. It's difficult to argue with him. To be fair, things likely would've been less miserable for him by now if it wasn't for the Astros playing the "In The Air Tonight" drum fill on a dugout trash can in Game 5 of the 2017 World Series, but we can't travel back in time or undo wrongs. All Kershaw can do next year is what he admirably does every year: give it another go and hope this time he'll be able to break his personal time loop.

YEAR	TEAM	LVL	AGE	WHIP	ERA	DRA	WARP	MPH	FB%	WHF	CSP
2017	LAN	MLB	29	0.95	2.31	2.24	6.5	94.8	47.8	15.3	46.5
2018	LAN	MLB	30	1.04	2.73	3.11	4.1	92.9	41.2	11.8	50.6
2019	LAN	MLB	31	1.04	3.03	3.33	4.7	91.9	43.9	14.3	46.4
2020	LAN	MLB	32	1.07	2.69	3.18	5.0	92.0	43.6	13.6	47.4

Los Angeles Dodgers 2020

Clayton Kershaw, continued

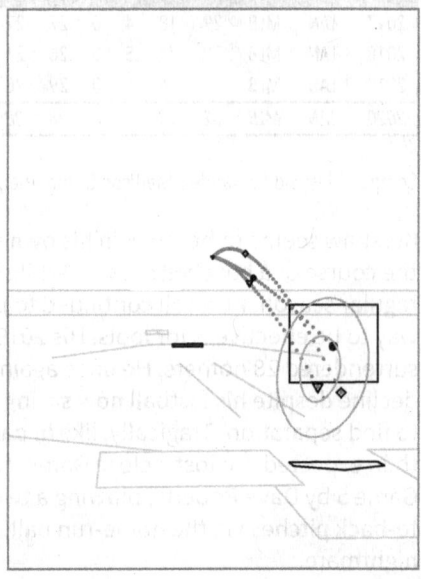

Type	Frequency	Velocity	H Movement	V Movement
● Fastball	43.8%	90.6 [95]	-0.7 [133]	-13 [108]
□ Sinker				
+ Cutter				
▲ Changeup				
✕ Splitter				
▽ Slider	39.1%	87.1 [111]	-3.8 [95]	-25.3 [123]
◇ Curveball	16.3%	73.7 [84]	-2.2 [79]	-60 [74]
⊕ Slow Curveball				
✻ Knuckleball				
▼ Screwball				

Adam Kolarek LHP

Born: 01/14/89 Age: 31 Bats: L Throws: L
Height: 6'3" Weight: 215 Origin: Round 11, 2010 Draft (#332 overall)

YEAR	TEAM	LVL	AGE	W	L	SV	G	GS	IP	H	HR	BB/9	K/9	K	GB%	BABIP
2017	DUR	AAA	28	3	4	2	41	0	43^2	37	0	3.3	9.5	46	74%	.311
2017	TBA	MLB	28	1	0	0	12	0	8^1	9	2	4.3	4.3	4	61%	.269
2018	DUR	AAA	29	5	1	4	31	1	44^2	35	1	2.4	10.5	52	64%	.306
2018	TBA	MLB	29	1	0	2	31	0	34^1	38	0	1.3	5.0	19	59%	.328
2019	TBA	MLB	30	4	3	1	54	0	43^1	39	6	2.9	7.5	36	65%	.264
2019	LAN	MLB	30	2	0	0	26	0	11^2	9	1	1.5	6.9	9	74%	.242
2020	LAN	MLB	31	2	2	0	48	0	50	53	8	2.9	7.3	41	63%	.298

Comparables: Hunter Cervenka, Kevin Chapman, Bobby LaFromboise

Kolarek quickly proved his worth to the Dodgers following his mid-season acquisition. While he had an unremarkable 3.95 ERA with a Rays team that let him face righties, the Dodgers promptly deployed him as their LOOGY and the results were amazing. Kolarek posted a 0.77 ERA in 11 2/3 innings, limiting lefties to a .370 OPS. Most importantly, in the biggest moments of his career, Kolarek dominated Juan Soto in the NLDS: facing the Nationals wunderkind three times, Kolarek didn't flinch, inducing a comebacker to go along with two strikeouts. Their fourth potential matchup (in Game 5) remains one of the greatest "what ifs" of the 2019 season, as the Nationals burned Clayton Kershaw twice and went on to win the series and the Series. On the strength of his excellent turn as a LOOGY, Kolarek should be an easy choice for the 2020 'pen. However, a likely rule change will force pitchers to face at least three hitters or end a half inning, making his roster spot (and career) and pretty big question mark unto itself.

YEAR	TEAM	LVL	AGE	WHIP	ERA	DRA	WARP	MPH	FB%	WHF	CSP
2017	DUR	AAA	28	1.21	1.65	3.84	0.7				
2017	TBA	MLB	28	1.56	6.48	8.19	-0.3	92.3	88.2	7.4	49.6
2018	DUR	AAA	29	1.05	1.61	2.91	1.1				
2018	TBA	MLB	29	1.25	3.93	4.25	0.3	93.2	63.7	10.1	53.4
2019	TBA	MLB	30	1.22	3.95	3.78	0.7	92.5	80.9	10.4	46.3
2019	LAN	MLB	30	0.94	0.77	3.81	0.2	91.4	83.2	16.8	47
2020	LAN	MLB	31	1.37	4.43	4.71	0.4	91.7	75.8	10.9	49.3

Los Angeles Dodgers 2020

Adam Kolarek, continued

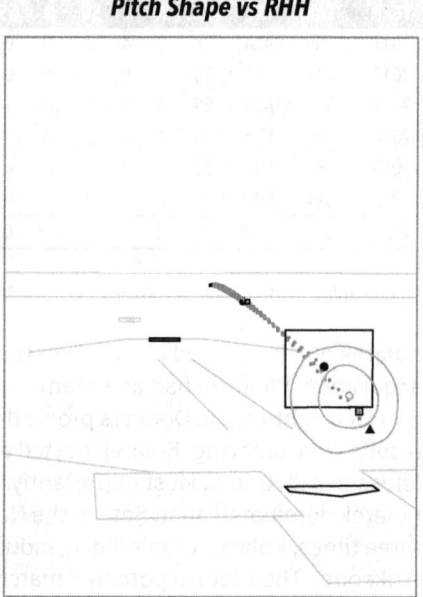

Type	Frequency	Velocity	H Movement	V Movement
● Fastball	10.6%	92 [99]	12.2 [76]	-17.3 [96]
☐ Sinker	70.8%	89.3 [83]	16.7 [74]	-34.8 [49]
+ Cutter				
▲ Changeup	9.7%	82.2 [89]	18 [68]	-39.3 [65]
✕ Splitter				
▽ Slider	8.9%	76.7 [68]	-6.6 [107]	-35.6 [93]
◇ Curveball				
⊕ Slow Curveball				
✳ Knuckleball				
▼ Screwball				

Dustin May   RHP

Born: 09/06/97   Age: 22   Bats: R   Throws: R
Height: 6'6"   Weight: 180   Origin: Round 3, 2016 Draft (#101 overall)

YEAR	TEAM	LVL	AGE	W	L	SV	G	GS	IP	H	HR	BB/9	K/9	K	GB%	BABIP
2017	GRL	A	19	9	6	0	23	23	123	121	8	1.9	8.3	113	52%	.306
2017	RCU	A+	19	0	0	0	2	1	11	6	0	0.8	12.3	15	60%	.240
2018	RCU	A+	20	7	3	0	17	17	98^1	91	9	1.6	8.6	94	58%	.294
2018	TUL	AA	20	2	2	0	6	6	34^1	27	0	3.1	7.3	28	54%	.267
2019	TUL	AA	21	3	5	0	15	15	79^1	71	5	2.3	9.8	86	52%	.307
2019	OKL	AAA	21	3	0	0	5	5	27^1	21	0	3.0	7.9	24	60%	.276
2019	LAN	MLB	21	2	3	0	14	4	34^2	33	2	1.3	8.3	32	46%	.316
2020	LAN	MLB	22	7	6	0	30	19	112	114	15	2.7	7.7	97	50%	.300

Comparables: José Berríos, Jake Thompson, Lucas Giolito

Some guy named Craig once said that May has extreme Waluigi energy, which is a perfect description of the gangly mannerisms of the top Dodgers pitching prospect. We knew about the glorious mane of red hair, but weren't prepared for how animated he is, portending aesthetic promise on top of athletic. Shuffling between 'pen and starting roles, May impressed with a 3.63 ERA and 2.90 FIP, while perhaps the most impressive thing about his debut was his walk rate of just 3.6 percent. He leans heavily on a sinker that moves like a mid-to-upper-90s changeup. His cutter, curve, and change all show signs of being usable pitches, but if he hopes to achieve his upside May will have to develop one of them into a consistent strikeout offering. That's easier said than done, but even in his current form his floor is a worthy rotation option, and May is an adjustment away from being a Dodgers mainstay. WAHHH!

YEAR	TEAM	LVL	AGE	WHIP	ERA	DRA	WARP	MPH	FB%	WHF	CSP
2017	GRL	A	19	1.20	3.88	4.28	1.4				
2017	RCU	A+	19	0.64	0.82	1.81	0.4				
2018	RCU	A+	20	1.10	3.29	2.98	2.7				
2018	TUL	AA	20	1.14	3.67	3.50	0.7				
2019	TUL	AA	21	1.15	3.74	3.84	1.1				
2019	OKL	AAA	21	1.10	2.30	1.90	1.3				
2019	LAN	MLB	21	1.10	3.63	4.55	0.4	98.1	57.2	9.7	52.1
2020	LAN	MLB	22	1.31	4.10	4.39	1.7	98.1	59.6	10.1	54.3

Los Angeles Dodgers 2020

Dustin May, continued

Pitch Shape vs LHH   **Pitch Shape vs RHH**

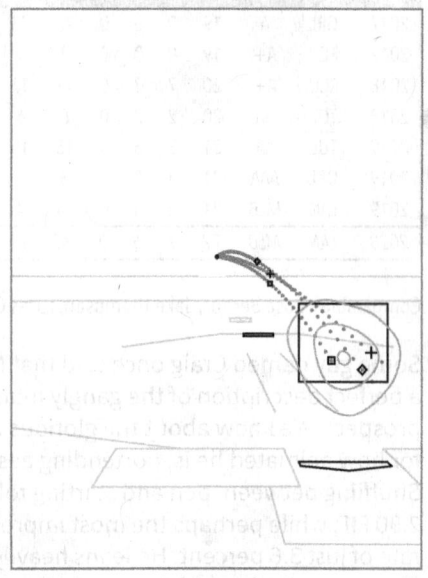

Type	Frequency	Velocity	H Movement	V Movement
● Fastball	6.9%	95.9 [110]	-6.7 [101]	-12.7 [108]
□ Sinker	50.4%	96.2 [119]	-14.6 [88]	-18.5 [107]
+ Cutter	29.5%	90.9 [114]	2 [101]	-24.2 [99]
▲ Changeup				
✕ Splitter				
▽ Slider				
◇ Curveball	10.6%	83.2 [115]	7.8 [101]	-47.5 [100]
◆ Slow Curveball				
✳ Knuckleball				
▼ Screwball				

Jimmy Nelson   RHP
Born: 06/05/89   Age: 31   Bats: R   Throws: R
Height: 6'6"   Weight: 250   Origin: Round 2, 2010 Draft (#64 overall)

YEAR	TEAM	LVL	AGE	W	L	SV	G	GS	IP	H	HR	BB/9	K/9	K	GB%	BABIP
2017	MIL	MLB	28	12	6	0	29	29	175^1	171	16	2.5	10.2	199	51%	.340
2019	SAN	AAA	30	3	2	0	16	4	40^1	33	4	5.4	12.7	57	43%	.322
2019	MIL	MLB	30	0	2	0	10	3	22	25	4	7.0	10.6	26	35%	.375
2020	LAN	MLB	31	2	2	0	33	0	35	35	5	4.2	8.6	33	42%	.299

Comparables: Rubby De La Rosa, Shane Greene, Joe Kelly

Nelson's 2019 season is why people push back against the tough guy culture that plagues baseball (and all professional sports). Nelson is known as one of the most competitive people in Milwaukee's organization, and he was itching to return as soon as possible after missing the entirety of 2018 due to a shoulder injury (suffered, of all things, running the bases). He was supposed to be healthy by spring training 2019, but setback after setback pushed his debut into June, and after three awful starts and a swift demotion to the bullpen, it was revealed that he had aggravated an elbow issue he had been dealing with since spring training. He obviously wasn't ready, but whether through his own bullheadedness or the Brewers' desperation for a top-flight starter, he was pushed through regardless. Nelson pitched all of 22 innings for the 2019 Brewers as a result of his boneheaded handling, and was non-tendered afterward.

YEAR	TEAM	LVL	AGE	WHIP	ERA	DRA	WARP	MPH	FB%	WHF	CSP
2017	MIL	MLB	28	1.25	3.49	3.32	4.4	95.9	61.2	12.3	50.7
2019	SAN	AAA	30	1.41	4.69	2.71	1.5				
2019	MIL	MLB	30	1.91	6.95	7.15	-0.4	94.8	52.1	10.4	44
2020	LAN	MLB	31	1.46	4.83	5.02	0.2	94.8	59.1	11.9	46.2

Los Angeles Dodgers 2020

Jimmy Nelson, continued

Pitch Shape vs LHH   **Pitch Shape vs RHH**

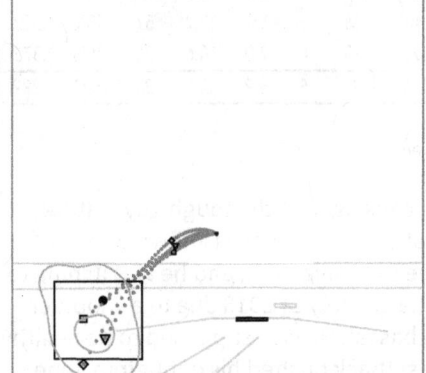
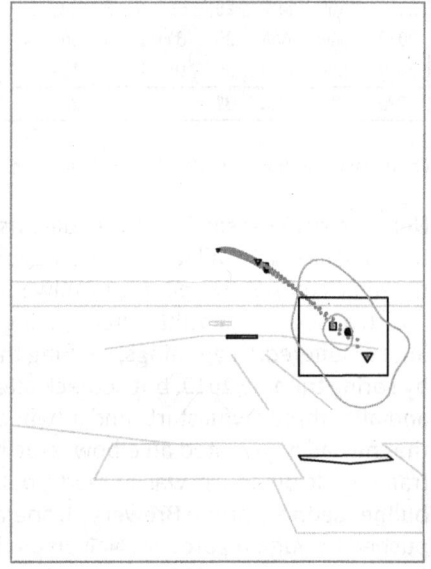

Type	Frequency	Velocity	H Movement	V Movement
● Fastball	24.7%	92.7 [101]	-0.3 [129]	-15.2 [102]
☐ Sinker	27.4%	93.3 [103]	-9 [123]	-19.1 [105]
+ Cutter				
▲ Changeup				
✕ Splitter				
▽ Slider	26.9%	85.7 [106]	11 [125]	-32.9 [100]
◇ Curveball	20.2%	83.1 [115]	9.5 [108]	-47.2 [101]
⊕ Slow Curveball				
✳ Knuckleball				
▼ Screwball				

David Price LHP

Born: 08/26/85 Age: 34 Bats: L Throws: L
Height: 6'5" Weight: 215 Origin: Round 1, 2007 Draft (#1 overall)

YEAR	TEAM	LVL	AGE	W	L	SV	G	GS	IP	H	HR	BB/9	K/9	K	GB%	BABIP
2017	BOS	MLB	31	6	3	0	16	11	74^2	65	8	2.9	9.2	76	40%	.278
2018	BOS	MLB	32	16	7	0	30	30	176	151	25	2.6	9.1	177	41%	.274
2019	BOS	MLB	33	7	5	0	22	22	107^1	109	15	2.7	10.7	128	42%	.336
2020	BOS	MLB	34	11	7	0	26	26	150	136	23	2.5	10.0	167	40%	.294

Comparables: Cole Hamels, Jon Lester, Gio Gonzalez

With Chris Sale and Nathan Eovaldi hurt, and Rick Porcello having one of his off years, the Red Sox turned to Price for an assist in carrying their rotation. He clearly misheard them, as the veteran lefty threw the second-fewest innings of his career thanks in large part to a cyst in his left wrist. If you're a Red Sox apologist, you could argue that 2019 was a lost season anyway, and that the Sox saved themselves from putting another 100-or-so innings on an arm to which they owe in excess of $60 million over the next three years. If you're more of a realist, you may point out that it's been three full seasons since the now 34-year-old Price has able to throw 200 innings. Price pitched quite well before the cyst started to limit his effectiveness in early July, and he had offseason surgery to remove the troublesome growth, so theoretically he should be at 100 percent come spring training. Yet, at this point even a Price who enters the year healthy can't be relied upon for 30-plus starts.

YEAR	TEAM	LVL	AGE	WHIP	ERA	DRA	WARP	MPH	FB%	WHF	CSP
2017	BOS	MLB	31	1.19	3.38	5.04	0.4	96.1	58.3	13.1	44.1
2018	BOS	MLB	32	1.14	3.58	3.72	3.2	94.6	46.5	10.8	49.9
2019	BOS	MLB	33	1.31	4.28	4.68	1.3	94.3	52	12.4	49.9
2020	BOS	MLB	34	1.18	3.59	3.86	2.8	93.6	49.7	11.6	47.7

David Price, continued

Pitch Shape vs LHH

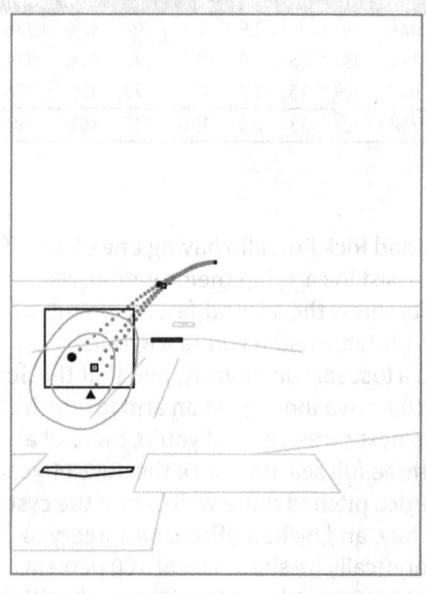

Pitch Shape vs RHH

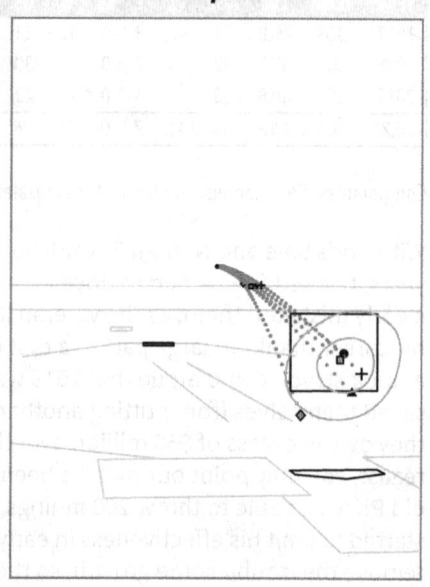

Type	Frequency	Velocity	H Movement	V Movement
● Fastball	23.8%	92.4 [100]	9.3 [89]	-15.6 [101]
□ Sinker	28.2%	92.2 [98]	14.6 [88]	-19.1 [104]
+ Cutter	19.7%	88.9 [102]	3.5 [68]	-22.5 [106]
▲ Changeup	25.8%	84.4 [97]	14.4 [85]	-29.8 [93]
✕ Splitter				
▽ Slider				
◇ Curveball				
⊕ Slow Curveball				
✳ Knuckleball				
▼ Screwball				

Josh Sborz   RHP
Born: 12/17/93   Age: 26   Bats: R   Throws: R
Height: 6'3"   Weight: 215   Origin: Round 2, 2015 Draft (#74 overall)

YEAR	TEAM	LVL	AGE	W	L	SV	G	GS	IP	H	HR	BB/9	K/9	K	GB%	BABIP
2017	TUL	AA	23	8	8	0	24	24	116^2	106	8	4.3	6.2	81	46%	.275
2018	TUL	AA	24	3	1	6	13	0	16^1	11	1	2.8	13.2	24	35%	.303
2018	OKL	AAA	24	1	1	0	33	0	37	38	0	3.6	11.4	47	43%	.388
2019	OKL	AAA	25	4	3	3	46	0	50	56	2	2.5	12.2	68	40%	.409
2019	LAN	MLB	25	0	1	0	7	0	9	10	2	4.0	7.0	7	38%	.296
2020	LAN	MLB	26	1	1	0	16	0	17	17	3	3.6	7.1	13	39%	.285

Comparables: Jacob Rhame, Hunter Wood, Tony Zych

The reality facing Sborz at the moment is that his results have never been all that good. He's relevant because over his minor-league career he's struck out around 12 and walked just three per nine. Add in a fastball that works from 94-96 mph and a slider and curve that both flash above-average, and there always seems to be a middle relief option in there. However, at 26, it does feel like Sborz needs to turn that promise into results sooner than later if he's to establish himself in a big-league pen, because the growing sample size of results is talking louder by the inning.

YEAR	TEAM	LVL	AGE	WHIP	ERA	DRA	WARP	MPH	FB%	WHF	CSP
2017	TUL	AA	23	1.39	3.86	4.74	0.6				
2018	TUL	AA	24	0.98	2.76	1.88	0.6				
2018	OKL	AAA	24	1.43	4.38	3.88	0.5				
2019	OKL	AAA	25	1.40	4.68	2.27	1.9				
2019	LAN	MLB	25	1.56	8.00	6.99	-0.2	96.4	64.3	10.8	44.9
2020	LAN	MLB	26	1.42	4.78	5.04	0.1	96.0	65.5	11	45.7

Los Angeles Dodgers 2020

Josh Sborz, continued

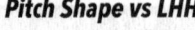
Pitch Shape vs LHH

Pitch Shape vs RHH

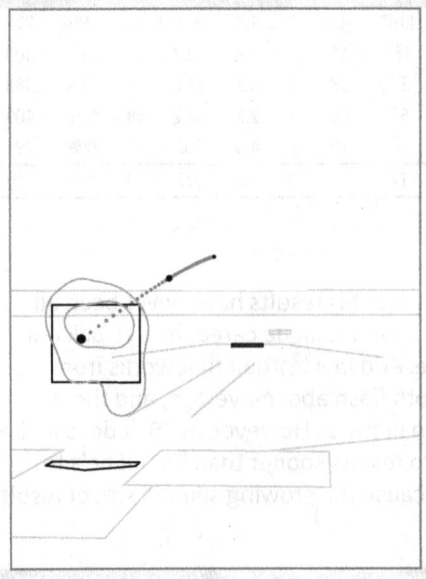
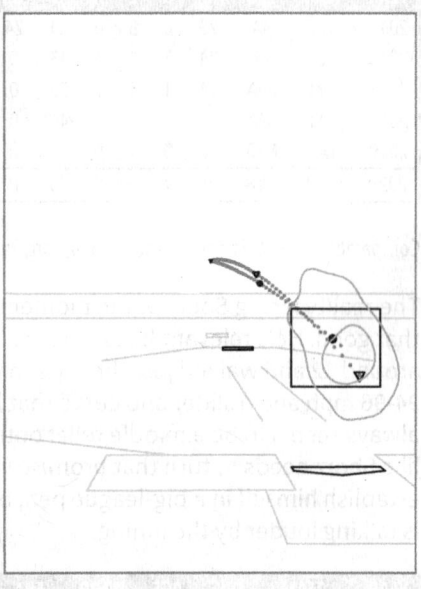

Type	Frequency	Velocity	H Movement	V Movement
● Fastball	64.3%	95.3 [108]	-3.5 [115]	-11.1 [113]
☐ Sinker				
+ Cutter				
▲ Changeup				
✕ Splitter				
▽ Slider	28.1%	86 [107]	2.2 [88]	-34.8 [95]
◇ Curveball	7.6%	78.3 [99]	6.9 [98]	-52 [91]
✦ Slow Curveball				
✻ Knuckleball				
▼ Screwball				

Ross Stripling   RHP

Born: 11/23/89   Age: 30   Bats: R   Throws: R
Height: 6'2"   Weight: 220   Origin: Round 5, 2012 Draft (#176 overall)

YEAR	TEAM	LVL	AGE	W	L	SV	G	GS	IP	H	HR	BB/9	K/9	K	GB%	BABIP
2017	LAN	MLB	27	3	5	2	49	2	74^1	69	10	2.3	9.0	74	51%	.294
2018	LAN	MLB	28	8	6	0	33	21	122	123	18	1.6	10.0	136	47%	.322
2019	LAN	MLB	29	4	4	0	32	15	90^2	84	11	2.0	9.2	93	51%	.299
2020	LAN	MLB	30	7	5	0	37	16	103	101	16	2.4	9.2	105	49%	.302

Comparables: Mike Fiers, Marco Estrada, Fernando Salas

It's easy to forget that the man nicknamed Chicken Strip was an All-Star as a starting pitcher in 2018, mainly because by the end of the year he was not only out of the rotation but off the playoff roster entirely. That early-'18 run represents his considerable upside, though, and his relegation to a swingman is more a testament to the Dodgers considerable depth than to Stripling's talents. Stripling has always been a good pitcher regardless of role, and nothing changed in that regard for 2019. It's easy to understand the team's reluctance to deal him given that he essentially functions as an insurance plan, but if another team correctly values him as a quality rotation arm, his best use to the Dodgers may be as a trade chip.

YEAR	TEAM	LVL	AGE	WHIP	ERA	DRA	WARP	MPH	FB%	WHF	CSP
2017	LAN	MLB	27	1.18	3.75	3.23	1.6	94.8	38.4	12	44.1
2018	LAN	MLB	28	1.19	3.02	2.94	3.3	94.3	41.1	12.5	47.3
2019	LAN	MLB	29	1.15	3.47	3.47	2.2	93.0	39	11.2	46.7
2020	LAN	MLB	30	1.24	3.73	4.12	1.8	93.1	39.7	11.9	46.1

Los Angeles Dodgers 2020

Ross Stripling, continued

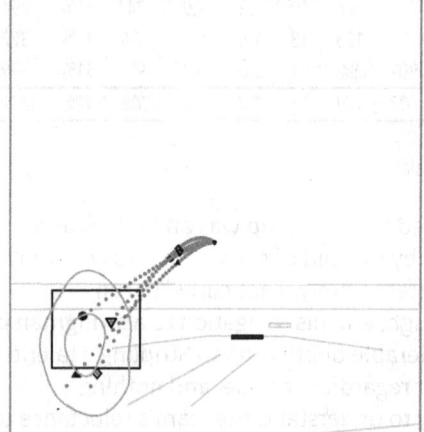
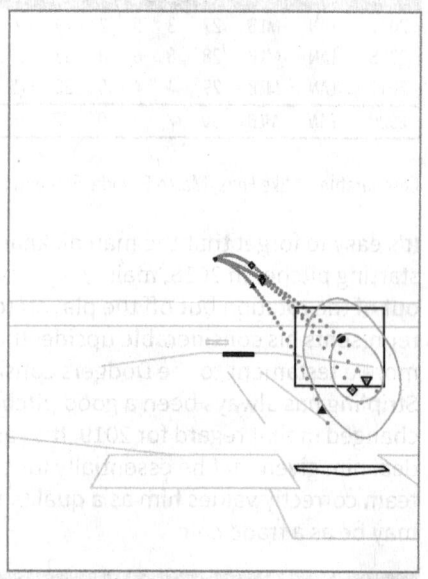

Type	Frequency	Velocity	H Movement	V Movement
● Fastball	37.3%	90.8 [95]	-2.5 [119]	-14 [105]
☐ Sinker				
+ Cutter				
▲ Changeup	14.7%	83 [92]	-7.5 [117]	-30.6 [91]
✕ Splitter				
▽ Slider	17.8%	86.7 [110]	4.5 [98]	-26.6 [119]
◇ Curveball	28.5%	80 [105]	5.3 [91]	-50.5 [94]
⊕ Slow Curveball				
✱ Knuckleball				
▼ Screwball				

Blake Treinen   RHP

Born: 06/30/88   Age: 32   Bats: R   Throws: R
Height: 6'5"   Weight: 225   Origin: Round 7, 2011 Draft (#226 overall)

YEAR	TEAM	LVL	AGE	W	L	SV	G	GS	IP	H	HR	BB/9	K/9	K	GB%	BABIP
2017	WAS	MLB	29	0	2	3	37	0	37^2	48	3	3.1	7.6	32	62%	.381
2017	OAK	MLB	29	3	4	13	35	0	38	32	3	2.8	9.9	42	60%	.299
2018	OAK	MLB	30	9	2	38	68	0	80^1	46	2	2.4	11.2	100	53%	.232
2019	OAK	MLB	31	6	5	16	57	0	58^2	58	9	5.7	9.1	59	45%	.306
2020	LAN	MLB	32	3	3	2	53	0	56	51	6	3.9	9.7	61	50%	.302

Comparables: Jeremy Jeffress, Ryan Tepera, Sam Dyson

For years, everyone wondered how batters could possibly touch Treinen's cocktail of wicked 99 mph two-seamers and vanishing offspeed pitches. For one year, they could not. In 2018, Treinen's sinker darted around and under barrels, he assumed the job as Oakland's closer and posted one of the best seasons we've seen out of a reliever in recent memory. The thing about cocktails is they can leave you with quite the hangover. In 2019, the right-hander battled through a couple minor ailments and lost a tick or two on his fastball, explaining his descent from Cy Young contender to replacement-level reliever as well as anything else. Rather than swing over sinking fastballs, hitters mostly laid off; in turn, Treinen's walk rate more than doubled and when he did come into the strike zone, opponents pounced, homering seven more times than they did a year ago. What awaits him in 2020? "Relievers are volatile" feels like a very 2015 bit of analysis, but it's a useful and truthful hedge in this case.

YEAR	TEAM	LVL	AGE	WHIP	ERA	DRA	WARP	MPH	FB%	WHF	CSP
2017	WAS	MLB	29	1.62	5.73	4.79	0.2	99.2	72.6	13.1	46.9
2017	OAK	MLB	29	1.16	2.13	3.96	0.5	99.4	61.8	14.3	48.3
2018	OAK	MLB	30	0.83	0.78	2.22	2.5	99.6	67.1	19.2	47.7
2019	OAK	MLB	31	1.62	4.91	5.64	-0.2	98.7	67.1	12.8	43.6
2020	LAN	MLB	32	1.35	3.72	3.98	0.9	98.2	66.5	15.2	45.5

Blake Treinen, continued

Pitch Shape vs LHH	Pitch Shape vs RHH
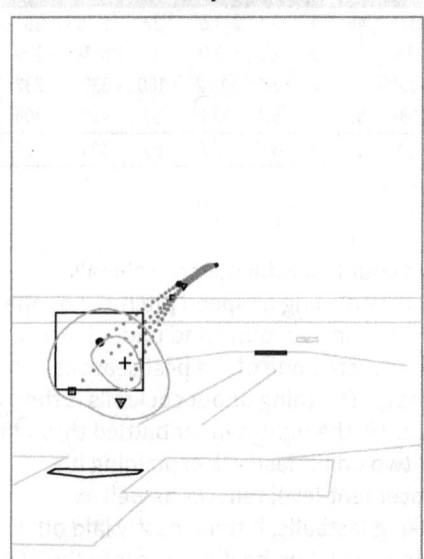	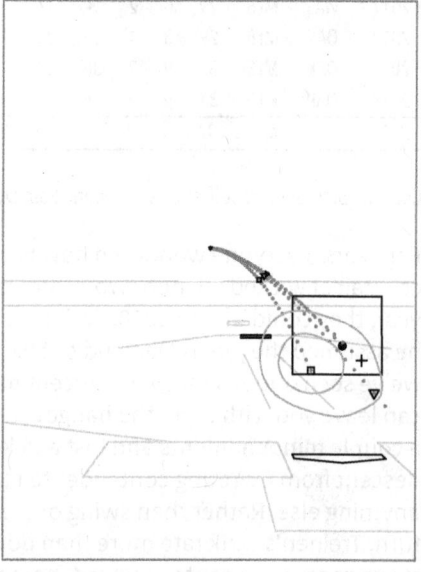

Type	Frequency	Velocity	H Movement	V Movement
● Fastball	21.7%	97.3 [114]	-10 [86]	-14.3 [104]
□ Sinker	45.4%	96.8 [122]	-16.1 [78]	-21.5 [96]
+ Cutter	18.8%	93.5 [130]	0.4 [91]	-20.8 [112]
▲ Changeup				
✕ Splitter				
▽ Slider	13.9%	88.6 [118]	3.3 [93]	-33.4 [99]
◇ Curveball				
◈ Slow Curveball				
✳ Knuckleball				
▼ Screwball				

Julio Urías   LHP

Born: 08/12/96 Age: 23 Bats: L Throws: L
Height: 6'0" Weight: 225 Origin: International Free Agent, 2012

YEAR	TEAM	LVL	AGE	W	L	SV	G	GS	IP	H	HR	BB/9	K/9	K	GB%	BABIP
2017	OKL	AAA	20	3	0	0	6	6	31^1	20	1	4.3	9.2	32	47%	.253
2017	LAN	MLB	20	0	2	0	5	5	23^1	23	1	5.4	4.2	11	43%	.293
2018	RCU	A+	21	0	0	0	4	4	7^1	6	3	4.9	16.0	13	46%	.300
2018	LAN	MLB	21	0	0	0	3	0	4	1	0	0.0	15.8	7	50%	.167
2019	LAN	MLB	22	4	3	4	37	8	79^2	59	7	3.1	9.6	85	39%	.257
2020	LAN	MLB	23	7	5	0	21	21	101	82	13	3.6	9.7	109	40%	.270

Comparables: Clayton Kershaw, Tyler Skaggs, Jose Rijo

Urías quickly became a fan favorite with the Dodgers, initially due to his phenom status after a meteoric rise through the minors to his big-league debut at 19, then due to his serious shoulder injury and journey back to the majors. But while the story of his 2019 should've been one of triumph over what could've been a career-derailing injury, one cannot talk about Urías in 2019 without mentioning his domestic violence suspension. The details are unfortunately still murky, but MLB saw fit to suspend him for 20 games and some wrongdoing on his part isn't in doubt. The Dodgers and Urías have thus far handled it reasonably well, but only time will tell if their actions will back up their words.

YEAR	TEAM	LVL	AGE	WHIP	ERA	DRA	WARP	MPH	FB%	WHF	CSP
2017	OKL	AAA	20	1.12	2.59	2.99	0.9				
2017	LAN	MLB	20	1.59	5.40	5.35	0.1	95.4	52	10.2	43.2
2018	RCU	A+	21	1.36	4.91	5.02	0.0				
2018	LAN	MLB	21	0.25	0.00	1.89	0.1	95.3	69	22.4	58.6
2019	LAN	MLB	22	1.08	2.49	3.39	1.8	97.1	60.3	15.3	45.7
2020	LAN	MLB	23	1.21	3.17	3.51	2.6	96.7	61.4	15.2	51.1

Julio Urías, continued

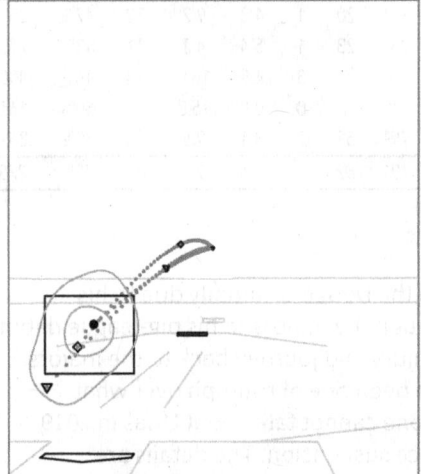
Pitch Shape vs LHH

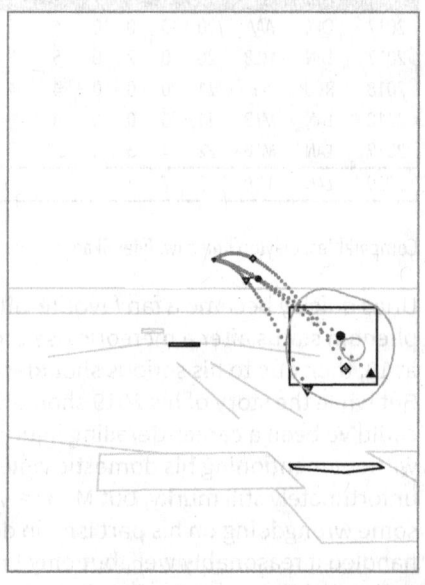
Pitch Shape vs RHH

Type	Frequency	Velocity	H Movement	V Movement
● Fastball	60.0%	95.3 [108]	2.4 [120]	-11.7 [111]
☐ Sinker				
+ Cutter				
▲ Changeup	16.3%	82.4 [90]	12.6 [94]	-26 [104]
✕ Splitter				
▽ Slider	17.3%	84.7 [101]	-4.4 [97]	-32.3 [102]
◇ Curveball	6.1%	77.4 [96]	-6 [94]	-48.8 [97]
✦ Slow Curveball				
✱ Knuckleball				
▼ Screwball				

Alex Wood   LHP

Born: 01/12/91 Age: 29 Bats: R Throws: L
Height: 6'4" Weight: 215 Origin: Round 2, 2012 Draft (#85 overall)

YEAR	TEAM	LVL	AGE	W	L	SV	G	GS	IP	H	HR	BB/9	K/9	K	GB%	BABIP
2017	LAN	MLB	26	16	3	0	27	25	152^1	123	15	2.2	8.9	151	54%	.267
2018	LAN	MLB	27	9	7	0	33	27	151^2	143	14	2.4	8.0	135	50%	.293
2019	CIN	MLB	28	1	3	0	7	7	35^2	41	11	2.3	7.6	30	39%	.294
2020	CIN	MLB	29	2	2	0	33	0	35	35	6	2.7	8.1	32	45%	.289

Comparables: David Price, Kevin Gausman, Gerrit Cole

People watch sports for different reasons. Some people love the puzzles of strategy and roster-building. Some people love that anything can happen at any time, no matter how unlikely. Others enjoy watching individual players overcome adversity and hearing those stories. Some just like the aesthetic splendor of seeing players with otherworldly physical gifts, mental acuity and work ethic perform almost absurd feats of skill and strength. Sadly, sometimes those physical gifts are bestowed on a body that can't hold up to the task of doing the very thing it is better than basically everyone else at doing it.

Wood's career isn't over by any means, but so far it has been a frustrating story. Wood flashes brilliance and uncorks multi-month stretches of dominance, only to break down from the repeated and unnatural act of pitching—a decay perhaps exacerbated by his unusual delivery. While in the past, Wood has muddled through to still wind up with strong numbers at the end of a mostly-complete season, 2019 was a lost year. He barely pitched and when he did he got smoked before getting shut down with a back injury. He continued to rehab but setbacks and the Reds' disappointing season kept him on the shelf. Hopefully an offseason to rest and heal will get Wood back to his effective self in 2020, so that we can enjoy his brilliance instead of the frustrating downside of his absence.

YEAR	TEAM	LVL	AGE	WHIP	ERA	DRA	WARP	MPH	FB%	WHF	CSP
2017	LAN	MLB	26	1.06	2.72	2.89	4.5	94.1	50.4	12.5	45.1
2018	LAN	MLB	27	1.21	3.68	3.41	3.3	91.9	43.1	11.6	47.2
2019	CIN	MLB	28	1.40	5.80	6.31	-0.2	91.3	50.3	12.1	45
2020	CIN	MLB	29	1.29	4.27	4.43	0.4	92.0	46.7	12	45.7

Los Angeles Dodgers 2020

Alex Wood, continued

Pitch Shape vs LHH   **Pitch Shape vs RHH**

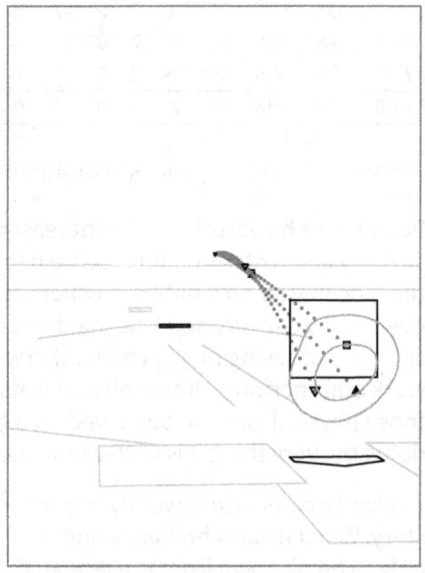

Type	Frequency	Velocity	H Movement	V Movement
● Fastball				
☐ Sinker	50.0%	90 [86]	12 [104]	-18.5 [106]
+ Cutter				
▲ Changeup	25.1%	83.6 [94]	12.7 [93]	-30.6 [91]
✕ Splitter				
▽ Slider	24.6%	81.3 [87]	-2.9 [91]	-39.7 [81]
◇ Curveball				
⊕ Slow Curveball				
✴ Knuckleball				
▼ Screwball				

PLAYER COMMENTS WITHOUT GRAPHS

Michael Busch 2B
Born: 11/09/97   Age: 22   Bats: L   Throws: R
Height: 6'0"   Weight: 207   Origin: Round 1, 2019 Draft (#31 overall)

YEAR	TEAM	LVL	AGE	PA	R	2B	3B	HR	RBI	BB	K	SB	CS	AVG/OBP/SLG
2020	LAN	MLB	22	251	23	11	1	6	25	19	68	2	1	.210/.283/.345

Comparables: Wilmer Difo, Josh Prince, Lane Adams

Busch was selected with one of the two first-round picks the Dodgers had in 2019. Despite playing mostly first base in college, the organization will try him at second base with an eye on getting the most out of his bat. While he had just 35 plate appearances split between Rookie and A levels (.496 OPS) this year, Busch was pushed to the Arizona Fall League where he put up a 1.007 OPS in 22 plate appearances. Reports on Busch's bat are promising, as he controls the strike zone well and makes a lot of quality contact to all fields thanks to his smooth left-handed stroke. The biggest question is whether he can actually handle the keystone in the majors. Early returns have been positive and he seems primed to become a part of the next wave in the Dodgers' talent pipeline.

YEAR	TEAM	LVL	AGE	PA	DRC+	VORP	BABIP	BRR	FRAA	WARP
2020	LAN	MLB	22	251	71	-1.4	.271	0.0	2B 0	-0.1

Diego Cartaya C

Born: 09/07/01 Age: 18 Bats: R Throws: R
Height: 6'2" Weight: 199 Origin: International Free Agent, 2018

YEAR	TEAM	LVL	AGE	PA	R	2B	3B	HR	RBI	BB	K	SB	CS	AVG/OBP/SLG
2019	DOD	RK	17	150	25	10	0	3	13	11	31	1	0	.296/.353/.437
2020	LAN	MLB	18	251	22	12	1	4	23	18	79	3	1	.225/.288/.339

Comparables: Francisco Mejía, Chris Marrero, Cheslor Cuthbert

Cartaya is 18 and hasn't made it out of the complex leagues, but he is starting to make it clear why the Dodgers signed him for $2.5 million in 2018. Cartaya's bat came alive in 2019, and most importantly scouts see him developing nicely behind the plate while having a mature feel for hitting. It's difficult to project Cartaya at his tender age, but the Dodgers are treating him like a potential starter. He'll likely be promoted next year, perhaps even to A-ball. Although his breakout as a prospect is likely a couple years off, it wouldn't surprise if he made the Dodgers reconsider their schedule.

YEAR	TEAM	LVL	AGE	PA	DRC+	VORP	BABIP	BRR	FRAA	WARP
2019	DOD	RK	17	150	126	12.3	.359	1.9	C(28): -0.2	1.1
2020	LAN	MLB	18	251	68	-2.3	.322	0.0	C 0	-0.2

Kody Hoese   3B

Born: 07/13/97   Age: 22   Bats: R   Throws: R
Height: 6'4"   Weight: 200   Origin: Round 1, 2019 Draft (#25 overall)

YEAR	TEAM	LVL	AGE	PA	R	2B	3B	HR	RBI	BB	K	SB	CS	AVG/OBP/SLG
2019	DOD	RK	21	68	14	5	1	3	13	10	11	1	0	.357/.456/.643
2019	GRL	A	21	103	15	3	1	2	16	8	14	0	0	.264/.330/.385
2020	LAN	MLB	22	251	22	11	1	5	24	16	60	2	1	.226/.283/.344

Comparables: Matt Thaiss, Hunter Dozier, Erik Komatsu

Until further notice, "Hoese" is pronounced "Hoe-Say" because quite frankly that is what we all deserve. Name aside, Hoese was one of the two first-round draft picks the Dodgers had in 2019. While Hoese is never going to be the rangiest third baseman, reports indicate that he has the athleticism and arm to stick at the position. Of course, the draw is his offensive upside, where he pairs a disciplined approach with usable power to all fields. Expect him to start 2020 at A-ball again, but given that he's already 22, the Dodgers will likely push him aggressively if he gets out of the blocks quickly.

YEAR	TEAM	LVL	AGE	PA	DRC+	VORP	BABIP	BRR	FRAA	WARP
2019	DOD	RK	21	68	185	11.1	.395	1.9	3B(6): -0.5	0.8
2019	GRL	A	21	103	103	3.6	.286	-0.2	3B(11): 0.7	0.3
2020	LAN	MLB	22	251	68	-2.4	.285	0.0	3B 0	-0.3

Connor Joe 1B

Born: 08/16/92 Age: 27 Bats: R Throws: R
Height: 6'0" Weight: 205 Origin: Round 1, 2014 Draft (#39 overall)

YEAR	TEAM	LVL	AGE	PA	R	2B	3B	HR	RBI	BB	K	SB	CS	AVG/OBP/SLG
2017	ALT	AA	24	282	29	11	4	5	30	34	40	2	4	.240/.338/.380
2017	MIS	AA	24	61	2	1	0	0	4	6	18	0	1	.135/.233/.154
2018	TUL	AA	25	248	35	16	1	11	30	38	57	1	2	.304/.425/.554
2018	OKL	AAA	25	188	34	10	2	6	25	22	31	2	0	.294/.385/.494
2019	OKL	AAA	26	446	82	26	1	15	68	72	81	1	2	.300/.426/.503
2019	SFN	MLB	26	16	1	0	0	0	0	1	5	0	0	.067/.125/.067
2020	LAN	MLB	27	251	27	9	1	7	28	28	59	1	0	.221/.319/.367

Comparables: Mike Ford, Tim Locastro, Mitch Haniger

The reigning king of having two traditionally first names made his major-league debut in 2019 following his 2018 breakout in the minors. Joe was selected in the Rule 5 Draft by the Reds from the Dodgers and then traded to the Giants. However, he was quickly designated for assignment and returned to the Dodgers after just 16 plate appearances in which he at least got his first (and only) big-league hit. Joe seemed undeterred as he put up another quality season in Triple-A as he waits in the wings for another cup of—no, we're not going to do it to you.

YEAR	TEAM	LVL	AGE	PA	DRC+	VORP	BABIP	BRR	FRAA	WARP
2017	ALT	AA	24	282	100	7.9	.266	1.5	RF(33): 0.5, 1B(24): 2.6	1.0
2017	MIS	AA	24	61	20	-4.2	.200	0.2	RF(11): 0.5, 1B(4): 0.4	-0.2
2018	TUL	AA	25	248	160	24.4	.375	1.2	3B(34): -1.7, 1B(21): -1.3	1.8
2018	OKL	AAA	25	188	127	10.7	.328	-0.2	1B(41): 0.5, 3B(4): -0.1	0.9
2019	OKL	AAA	26	446	137	33.8	.347	0.1	1B(78): -1.1, LF(10): -0.2	2.4
2019	SFN	MLB	26	16	59	-0.4	.100	0.0	LF(5): 2.2	0.2
2020	LAN	MLB	27	251	86	3.1	.268	-0.4	1B 2, RF 0	0.5

Gavin Lux SS

Born: 11/23/97 Age: 22 Bats: L Throws: R
Height: 6'2" Weight: 190 Origin: Round 1, 2016 Draft (#20 overall)

YEAR	TEAM	LVL	AGE	PA	R	2B	3B	HR	RBI	BB	K	SB	CS	AVG/OBP/SLG
2017	GRL	A	19	501	68	14	8	7	39	56	88	27	10	.244/.331/.362
2018	RCU	A+	20	404	64	23	7	11	48	43	68	11	7	.324/.396/.520
2018	TUL	AA	20	120	21	4	1	4	9	14	20	2	2	.324/.408/.495
2019	TUL	AA	21	291	45	7	4	13	37	28	60	7	3	.313/.375/.521
2019	OKL	AAA	21	232	54	18	4	13	39	33	42	3	3	.392/.478/.719
2019	LAN	MLB	21	82	12	4	1	2	9	7	24	2	0	.240/.305/.400
2020	LAN	MLB	22	392	46	18	3	14	51	34	100	6	3	.267/.333/.454

Comparables: Corey Seager, Brendan Rodgers, Dilson Herrera

It seems like eons ago that Lux struggled mightily to hit in A-ball, but that it was just a couple years back proves the mantra that development isn't linear. After his breakout last year, Lux continued to cement his lofty prospect status in Double-A. Lux burned brightest following his promotion to Oklahoma City, when he went all Barry Bonds on the PCL, a performance that propelled him to becoming Dodgers Minor League Player Of The Year, a consensus top-five overall prospect ranking, and a big-league debut. The team appeared reluctant to promote him ahead of schedule, but Lux forced their hand. His overall line in the majors was unimpressive, but he demonstrated flashes of the star quality that has the team so optimistic about his future. Most importantly, he looks like the antagonist jock of every heartwarming teen movie, which will only increase the entertainment value of everything he does.

YEAR	TEAM	LVL	AGE	PA	DRC+	VORP	BABIP	BRR	FRAA	WARP
2017	GRL	A	19	501	97	20.4	.288	3.4	SS(65): 3.8, 2B(43): 4.0	2.8
2018	RCU	A+	20	404	144	34.4	.374	-1.8	SS(66): -0.6, 2B(17): 0.8	3.2
2018	TUL	AA	20	120	153	11.6	.370	1.3	SS(26): -0.6	1.2
2019	TUL	AA	21	291	166	28.9	.358	-2.6	SS(55): -3.0, 2B(7): 0.5	2.4
2019	OKL	AAA	21	232	176	41.2	.451	-1.2	SS(35): -2.8, 2B(12): -0.3	2.7
2019	LAN	MLB	21	82	75	0.1	.327	0.1	2B(22): -0.9	-0.1
2020	LAN	MLB	22	392	107	19.2	.334	-0.1	2B 0	2.0

DJ Peters CF

Born: 12/12/95 Age: 24 Bats: R Throws: R
Height: 6'6" Weight: 225 Origin: Round 4, 2016 Draft (#131 overall)

YEAR	TEAM	LVL	AGE	PA	R	2B	3B	HR	RBI	BB	K	SB	CS	AVG/OBP/SLG
2017	RCU	A+	21	587	91	29	5	27	82	64	189	3	3	.276/.372/.514
2018	TUL	AA	22	559	79	23	3	29	60	45	192	1	2	.236/.320/.473
2019	TUL	AA	23	288	31	10	1	11	42	28	93	1	0	.241/.331/.422
2019	OKL	AAA	23	255	40	10	1	12	39	33	75	1	1	.260/.388/.490
2020	LAN	MLB	24	251	25	10	1	7	27	21	91	0	0	.209/.293/.355

Comparables: Ryan O'Hearn, Joe Benson, Brett Jackson

At 6-foot-6 and 230 pounds, Peters looks the part of a top prospect, with a beefier Jayson Werth an understandable comp for dreamers. The raw power is the athletic outfielder's calling card and the Dodgers are working hard to find him a swing that can tap into that as often as possible. Peters flashed big power in 2018 but was otherwise too easy of an out at the plate, racking up monster strikeout totals without the walks to balance them. He made progress this year, cutting down on the whiffs and upping the walks, with only a slight reduction in his home run totals. He'll need that trend to continue in the right direction to attain a big-league future, with his contact rate representing a significant hurdle to overcome. He'll head back to Triple-A as he continues to iron out the kinks in his swing, and consistently produce more quality plate appearances.

YEAR	TEAM	LVL	AGE	PA	DRC+	VORP	BABIP	BRR	FRAA	WARP
2017	RCU	A+	21	587	118	43.2	.385	0.9	CF(80): -3.5, LF(18): -1.0	2.3
2018	TUL	AA	22	559	97	20.6	.316	-3.6	CF(96): -3.1, RF(29): 1.4	0.9
2019	TUL	AA	23	288	104	15.7	.331	-0.6	CF(48): -1.2, RF(20): 1.1	0.9
2019	OKL	AAA	23	255	120	19.6	.341	0.0	CF(55): -0.9	1.4
2020	LAN	MLB	24	251	74	-0.8	.316	-0.3	CF -1, RF 0	-0.1

Luis Rodriguez OF
Born: 09/16/02 Age: 17 Bats: R Throws: R
Height: 6'2" Weight: 175 Origin: International Free Agent, 2019

Rodriguez is a 17-year-old outfielder from Venezuela who has yet to play an inning of professional baseball but was highly ranked in the 2019 July 2nd market. At 6-foot-2, Rodriguez has a lot of projection and pairs that with athleticism and instincts to provide a foundation for evaluators to dream on. Whether he's able to stick in center field will depend on how he fills out, but one thing that's agreed upon is his ability with a bat in his hand. He pairs impressive bat speed with an ability to consistently find the sweet spot. Wild speculation and dreaming big are always fun, but the basic report provided above has been written about any number of prospect shortly after they signed as teenagers. A little caution would be the prudent approach as it pertains to his prospect status.

Keibert Ruiz C

Born: 07/20/98 Age: 21 Bats: B Throws: R
Height: 6'0" Weight: 200 Origin: International Free Agent, 2015

YEAR	TEAM	LVL	AGE	PA	R	2B	3B	HR	RBI	BB	K	SB	CS	AVG/OBP/SLG
2017	GRL	A	18	251	34	16	1	2	24	18	30	0	0	.317/.372/.423
2017	RCU	A+	18	160	24	7	1	6	27	7	23	0	0	.315/.344/.497
2018	TUL	AA	19	415	44	14	0	12	47	26	33	0	1	.268/.328/.401
2019	TUL	AA	20	310	33	9	0	4	25	28	21	0	0	.254/.329/.330
2019	OKL	AAA	20	40	6	0	0	2	9	2	1	0	0	.316/.350/.474
2020	LAN	MLB	21	35	4	2	0	1	4	2	5	0	0	.259/.311/.394

Comparables: Jake Bauers, Jose Tabata, Wilmer Flores

Was there a trade package involving the Dodgers for the last year or so that Ruiz was not a part of? That must've been mighty annoying for a player who was once the prize of the system and was assumed to be the future starter. With Will Smith's ascendance,

YEAR	TEAM	P. COUNT	FRM RUNS	BLK RUNS	THRW RUNS	TOT RUNS
2018	TUL	11928	5.3	-0.6	-0.4	3.9
2019	OKL	1280	-0.3	0.0	0.0	0.4
2019	TUL	8565	3.3	0.0	-2.2	1.0
2020	LAN	1280	-0.2	0.0	-0.1	-0.3

Ruiz is in a bit of a no man's land within the organization. Ruiz has stagnated in the upper minors. Still just 20 years old, he's struggled to turn his sub-seven percent whiff rate into useful production. The offensive bar for catchers is essentially resting on the floor, but the promise that Ruiz once showed in his ability to marry power with contact his dissipated. Reports still indicate that a top prospect's tools reside within Ruiz's frame, but descriptive words being used are a bit more muted and hesitant than they were in recent memory.

YEAR	TEAM	LVL	AGE	PA	DRC+	VORP	BABIP	BRR	FRAA	WARP
2017	GRL	A	18	251	127	16.2	.355	-3.2	C(49): -0.9	1.3
2017	RCU	A+	18	160	127	13.2	.333	0.0	C(37): -0.3	1.2
2018	TUL	AA	19	415	91	8.3	.266	-3.8	C(86): 3.5	1.4
2019	TUL	AA	20	310	105	4.1	.261	-3.5	C(61): 0.5	1.1
2019	OKL	AAA	20	40	87	-0.5	.286	0.9	C(8): -0.5	0.2
2020	LAN	MLB	21	35	86	0.9	.279	-0.1	C 0	0.1

Edwin Ríos CI

Born: 04/21/94 Age: 26 Bats: L Throws: R
Height: 6'3" Weight: 220 Origin: Round 6, 2015 Draft (#192 overall)

YEAR	TEAM	LVL	AGE	PA	R	2B	3B	HR	RBI	BB	K	SB	CS	AVG/OBP/SLG
2017	TUL	AA	23	332	47	21	0	15	62	17	69	1	1	.317/.358/.533
2017	OKL	AAA	23	190	23	13	0	9	29	18	42	0	1	.296/.368/.533
2018	OKL	AAA	24	341	45	25	0	10	55	23	110	0	1	.304/.355/.482
2019	OKL	AAA	25	444	72	23	2	31	91	37	153	2	2	.270/.340/.575
2019	LAN	MLB	25	56	10	2	1	4	8	9	21	0	0	.277/.393/.617
2020	LAN	MLB	26	77	8	4	0	3	10	5	29	0	0	.227/.287/.414

Comparables: Chris Shaw, Ryan O'Hearn, Tyler Austin

Seemingly destined to be a bat-only Quad-A type, Ríos got his shot with the Dodgers towards the end of June and ran with it. He put an exclamation point on his season by smashing the longest home run by a Dodger (473 feet) on a team that led the NL in homers by a significant margin. Any GM of a rebuilding club watching the endless parade of bats breaking out for the Dodgers has to try and pry a guy like Ríos away with the idea of giving him a shot at being a regular, right? The Dodgers don't have room for him, and the elevated strikeout rates make him a risk, but there's no reason he couldn't have a late breakout like other Dodgers before him.

YEAR	TEAM	LVL	AGE	PA	DRC+	VORP	BABIP	BRR	FRAA	WARP
2017	TUL	AA	23	332	144	24.9	.363	0.9	3B(38): -4.1, 1B(28): 1.8	2.0
2017	OKL	AAA	23	190	121	8.6	.345	-2.6	1B(33): 0.6, 3B(9): -1.0	0.6
2018	OKL	AAA	24	341	116	16.6	.433	-2.4	3B(38): -4.2, 1B(28): -1.3	0.6
2019	OKL	AAA	25	444	106	24.4	.349	-2.6	3B(66): 1.7, 1B(25): 0.6	1.8
2019	LAN	MLB	25	56	87	0.5	.409	-0.2	1B(12): -0.4, 3B(5): -0.5	-0.1
2020	LAN	MLB	26	77	81	-0.1	.337	-0.2	LF 1, 1B 0	0.1

Miguel Vargas 3B

Born: 11/17/99 Age: 20 Bats: R Throws: R
Height: 6'3" Weight: 205 Origin: International Free Agent, 2017

YEAR	TEAM	LVL	AGE	PA	R	2B	3B	HR	RBI	BB	K	SB	CS	AVG/OBP/SLG
2018	DOD	RK	18	37	6	3	1	0	2	5	3	1	0	.419/.514/.581
2018	OGD	RK	18	103	25	11	1	2	22	8	13	6	1	.394/.447/.596
2018	GRL	A	18	89	4	1	1	0	6	10	20	0	0	.213/.307/.253
2019	GRL	A	19	323	53	20	2	5	45	35	43	9	1	.325/.399/.464
2019	RCU	A+	19	236	23	18	1	2	32	20	40	4	3	.284/.353/.408
2020	LAN	MLB	20	251	25	14	1	5	26	20	51	1	0	.259/.324/.393

Comparables: Jeimer Candelario, Delino DeShields, J.P. Crawford

Vargas defected from Cuba in 2015 and signed with the Dodgers in 2017 for $300,000. He quickly proved a wise investment for the team, as he impressed between Low-A and High-A with a combined .308/.380/.440 slash line. Vargas will likely be assigned back to Rancho Cucamonga in 2020 with an eye on a promotion to Tulsa if he starts out well. Scouts report Vargas is in possession of a discerning eye and an exceptional hit tool. While he doesn't show present power there's certainly room in his frame for him to develop some thump. Whether he sticks at third or not isn't yet clear, but his future will mostly be determined by the development of his bat.

YEAR	TEAM	LVL	AGE	PA	DRC+	VORP	BABIP	BRR	FRAA	WARP
2018	DOD	RK	18	37	196	4.6	.464	-0.7	1B(5): 0.8, 3B(4): 1.1	0.5
2018	OGD	RK	18	103	203	13.0	.443	1.2	3B(13): 0.5, 1B(6): -0.4	1.2
2018	GRL	A	18	89	66	-1.0	.281	-0.5	3B(19): 3.1	0.2
2019	GRL	A	19	323	162	27.6	.363	-2.5	3B(59): 2.2, 1B(2): 0.4	3.1
2019	RCU	A+	19	236	127	8.9	.341	-2.3	3B(43): -1.9, 1B(6): 0.4	0.8
2020	LAN	MLB	20	251	91	5.0	.314	-0.3	3B 0, 1B 0	0.5

Gerardo Carrillo   RHP

Born: 09/13/98   Age: 21   Bats: R   Throws: R
Height: 5'10"   Weight: 154   Origin: International Free Agent, 2016

YEAR	TEAM	LVL	AGE	W	L	SV	G	GS	IP	H	HR	BB/9	K/9	K	GB%	BABIP
2017	DDG	RK	18	5	2	0	14	10	48[1]	44	1	2.6	6.0	32	58%	.277
2018	DOD	RK	19	2	0	1	4	1	11	6	0	1.6	10.6	13	58%	.231
2018	GRL	A	19	2	1	0	9	9	49	35	3	2.8	6.8	37	50%	.235
2019	RCU	A+	20	5	9	0	23	21	86	87	3	5.3	9.0	86	54%	.338
2020	LAN	MLB	21	2	2	0	33	0	35	34	5	3.8	7.0	27	48%	.283

Comparables: Jeanmar Gómez, Lance McCullers Jr., German Márquez

Carrillo is all about velocity, which only popped up in recent years and has led to his sudden ascent as a prospect. When the 21-year-old Mexican is right, he's in the mid-90s with sink and velocity that has touched triple digits. His slider is his best secondary option and his curve flashes usable but lags behind. All of this makes relieving a realistic fallback option, especially when combined with his (lack of) height. Despite struggling to a mid-5s ERA in High-A, scouts remain high on his potential. Carrillo showcased his upside in the Arizona Fall League recently, posting a 2.22 ERA in 24 1/3 innings with 25 strikeouts against much more advanced competition. Based on results, he seems like an unlikely candidate to be a fast mover, but it wouldn't be surprising to see Carrillo get time in Tulsa next year as the Dodgers appear impressed.

YEAR	TEAM	LVL	AGE	WHIP	ERA	DRA	WARP	MPH	FB%	WHF	CSP
2017	DDG	RK	18	1.20	2.79	5.23	0.4				
2018	DOD	RK	19	0.73	0.82	1.71	0.5				
2018	GRL	A	19	1.02	1.65	3.26	1.1				
2019	RCU	A+	20	1.60	5.44	5.22	-0.2				
2020	LAN	MLB	21	1.41	4.63	4.85	0.2				

Josiah Gray RHP

Born: 12/21/97 Age: 22 Bats: R Throws: R
Height: 6'1" Weight: 190 Origin: Round 2, 2018 Draft (#72 overall)

YEAR	TEAM	LVL	AGE	W	L	SV	G	GS	IP	H	HR	BB/9	K/9	K	GB%	BABIP
2018	GRV	RK	20	2	2	0	12	12	52^1	29	1	2.9	10.1	59	38%	.219
2019	GRL	A	21	1	0	0	5	5	23^1	13	0	2.7	10.0	26	41%	.241
2019	RCU	A+	21	7	0	0	12	12	67^1	52	3	1.7	10.7	80	40%	.292
2019	TUL	AA	21	3	2	0	9	8	39^1	33	0	2.5	9.4	41	35%	.314
2020	LAN	MLB	22	1	1	0	11	0	11	11	2	3.2	8.9	11	38%	.302

Comparables: Chance Adams, Rafael Montero, Jorge Alcala

The other half of the prospect haul acquired for Yasiel Puig, Gray ended up as the team's Minor League Pitcher Of The Year. He plowed through three levels in 2019, ending his season in Double-A, posting a combined 2.28 ERA along the way. In 130 innings, he struck out an impressive 147 and walked just 31. While he can top out at 97 mph, he generally works in the low-to-mid 90s, adding to his swing-and-miss slider with a curve and change, both of which he's still trying to develop into legit third offerings. Gray is also a strike thrower, and both his relative inexperience (converted shortstop) and athleticism bode well for his fine command to come along eventually. It wouldn't be surprising if he makes himself relevant to the Dodgers bullpen in the second half of 2020.

YEAR	TEAM	LVL	AGE	WHIP	ERA	DRA	WARP	MPH	FB%	WHF	CSP
2018	GRV	RK	20	0.88	2.58	0.91	2.9				
2019	GRL	A	21	0.86	1.93	2.26	0.8				
2019	RCU	A+	21	0.97	2.14	2.29	2.2				
2019	TUL	AA	21	1.12	2.75	3.27	0.8				
2020	LAN	MLB	22	1.33	3.97	4.36	0.1				

Michael Grove   RHP

Born: 12/18/96   Age: 23   Bats: R   Throws: R
Height: 6'3"   Weight: 200   Origin: Round 2, 2018 Draft (#68 overall)

YEAR	TEAM	LVL	AGE	W	L	SV	G	GS	IP	H	HR	BB/9	K/9	K	GB%	BABIP
2019	RCU	A+	22	0	5	0	21	21	51^2	61	7	3.3	12.7	73	30%	.412
2020	LAN	MLB	23	2	2	0	33	0	35	36	6	4.2	10.0	39	32%	.323

Comparables: Mike Mayers, Taylor Williams, Zach Stewart

The Dodgers took a risk on Grove in 2018, selecting him in the second round despite the fact that he missed the whole year with Tommy John surgery. From a results perspective, the outcome hasn't paid off yet as he was assigned to High-A, where he struggled mightily in terms of surface stats. His peripherals fared much better, as he missed bats with frequency and recorded a solid walk rate. One thing to keep an eye on: The Cal League is a hitter's haven, Grove operates as a fly ball pitcher—it's possible he'll see markedly different topline stats in a more neutral environment. Perhaps most importantly, reports on Grove are that he's healthy again. He's once again seeing his pre-surgery velocity and stuff, sitting 92-94 mph with an above-average slider. The changeup still needs work, but given that he missed a year of development, that's not surprising. Still, he'll be 23 next year so the Dodgers likely want to push him to the upper minors with hopes that everything will come together. Being two years removed from the injury sets Grove up nicely for a breakout year.

YEAR	TEAM	LVL	AGE	WHIP	ERA	DRA	WARP	MPH	FB%	WHF	CSP
2019	RCU	A+	22	1.55	6.10	5.38	-0.2				
2020	LAN	MLB	23	1.50	4.99	5.18	0.1				

Dennis Santana RHP

Born: 04/12/96 Age: 24 Bats: R Throws: R
Height: 6'2" Weight: 190 Origin: International Free Agent, 2013

YEAR	TEAM	LVL	AGE	W	L	SV	G	GS	IP	H	HR	BB/9	K/9	K	GB%	BABIP
2017	RCU	A+	21	5	6	0	17	14	85.2	87	5	2.3	9.7	92	50%	.340
2017	TUL	AA	21	3	1	0	7	7	32.2	32	2	6.3	10.2	37	52%	.337
2018	TUL	AA	22	0	2	0	8	8	38.2	26	3	3.3	11.9	51	56%	.258
2018	OKL	AAA	22	1	1	0	2	2	11	10	0	1.6	11.5	14	45%	.345
2018	LAN	MLB	22	1	0	0	1	0	3.2	6	0	2.5	9.8	4	31%	.462
2019	OKL	AAA	23	5	9	0	27	17	93.1	111	16	5.1	10.1	105	44%	.364
2019	LAN	MLB	23	0	0	0	3	0	5	6	1	7.2	10.8	6	47%	.357
2020	LAN	MLB	24	3	2	0	17	6	44	38	6	4.5	9.5	46	43%	.281

Comparables: Touki Toussaint, Rob Whalen, Miguel Almonte

It was only 2018 when Santana seemed like the next pitcher up in the Dodgers system, popping up onto radars everywhere with an uptick in velocity and his swing-and-miss stuff. It seemed like 2019 would be the year to look for his true arrival in the majors. Instead, disaster struck: He maintained his ability to induce whiffs, but lost the strikezone entirely. Santana did make a cameo in the big leagues but did himself no favors there, either. Rather, he seemed to cement a relief role for himself if he was to return to the 25-man roster. That's a lot of negativity, but it's important to remember that he will be just 24 next season, so there's still time for him to right the ship. The Dodgers need relief help in 2020 and with an off-season to focus on his new role, they have to be hoping that Santana is one of the names that emerges.

YEAR	TEAM	LVL	AGE	WHIP	ERA	DRA	WARP	MPH	FB%	WHF	CSP
2017	RCU	A+	21	1.27	3.57	3.88	1.3				
2017	TUL	AA	21	1.68	5.51	4.93	0.1				
2018	TUL	AA	22	1.03	2.56	2.44	1.3				
2018	OKL	AAA	22	1.09	2.45	2.93	0.3				
2018	LAN	MLB	22	1.91	12.27	3.78	0.0	95.9	54.3	14.3	44.3
2019	OKL	AAA	23	1.76	6.94	6.51	0.1				
2019	LAN	MLB	23	2.00	7.20	5.24	0.0	94.6	56.7	13.5	39
2020	LAN	MLB	24	1.38	4.14	4.33	0.7	94.9	57.6	14.2	42.6

Mitchell White RHP

Born: 12/28/94   Age: 25   Bats: R   Throws: R
Height: 6'3"   Weight: 210   Origin: Round 2, 2016 Draft (#65 overall)

YEAR	TEAM	LVL	AGE	W	L	SV	G	GS	IP	H	HR	BB/9	K/9	K	GB%	BABIP
2017	DOD	RK	22	0	0	0	3	3	7	2	0	2.6	10.3	8	53%	.133
2017	RCU	A+	22	2	1	0	9	9	38^2	26	0	3.7	11.4	49	64%	.286
2017	TUL	AA	22	1	1	0	7	7	28	17	2	4.2	10.0	31	51%	.217
2018	TUL	AA	23	6	7	0	22	22	105^1	114	12	2.9	7.5	88	49%	.317
2019	TUL	AA	24	1	0	0	7	7	30	18	3	2.1	11.1	37	43%	.217
2019	OKL	AAA	24	3	6	0	16	13	63^2	73	13	3.4	9.6	68	43%	.349
2020	LAN	MLB	25	2	2	0	15	5	33	33	6	3.7	8.9	33	43%	.302

Comparables: Hunter Wood, Ben Lively, Jerad Eickhoff

White's upside continue to allure, as the 24-year-old can show a mid-90s fastball with movement, a wipeout slider that locks in strikeouts, and can really spin a curve. While not the most consistent strike-thrower, White finds the zone when necessary as well. Yet, in four years, he's thrown under 300 innings and carries an unremarkable 3.97 career ERA, so something has to give. After a promising start to the season in Double-A, he was promoted to Triple-A and struggled with the juiced ball. Through it all, White's peripherals have remained promising, which is what keeps the Dodgers clinging to a potential quality mid-rotation arm. However, given issues fighting his delivery, bouts with inconsistency, and injury woes, White fits the profile of a future relief arm and likely finds his calling there at some point.

YEAR	TEAM	LVL	AGE	WHIP	ERA	DRA	WARP	MPH	FB%	WHF	CSP
2017	DOD	RK	22	0.57	0.00	0.72	0.4				
2017	RCU	A+	22	1.09	3.72	2.41	1.3				
2017	TUL	AA	22	1.07	2.57	2.83	0.8				
2018	TUL	AA	23	1.41	4.53	5.57	-0.3				
2019	TUL	AA	24	0.83	2.10	2.97	0.7				
2019	OKL	AAA	24	1.52	6.50	4.94	1.0				
2020	LAN	MLB	25	1.41	4.55	4.84	0.3				

Los Angeles Dodgers 2020

LINEOUTS

Hitters

HITTER	POS	TEAM	LVL	AGE	PA	R	2B	3B	HR	RBI	BB	K	SB	CS	AVG/OBP/SLG	DRC+	WARP
Jacob Amaya	SS	RCU	A+	20	89	14	3	2	1	13	7	15	1	3	.250/.307/.375	99	0.2
	SS	GRL	A	20	470	68	25	4	6	58	74	83	4	4	.262/.381/.394	146	3.6
Austin Barnes	C	OKL	AAA	29	104	19	6	0	6	17	14	20	1	1	.264/.375/.540	104	0.6
	C	LAN	MLB	29	242	28	12	1	5	25	23	56	3	0	.203/.293/.340	78	1.6
Omar Estevez	2B	TUL	AA	21	336	34	24	0	6	36	31	70	0	2	.291/.352/.431	118	1.3
Jedd Gyorko	3B	LAN	MLB	30	39	1	1	0	0	2	3	10	0	0	.139/.205/.167	53	-0.1
	3B	SLN	MLB	30	62	5	0	0	2	7	6	14	2	0	.196/.274/.304	78	0.1
	3B	OKL	AAA	30	26	5	1	0	1	5	3	5	0	0	.273/.385/.455	90	-0.1
Jeren Kendall	CF	RCU	A+	23	412	51	11	10	19	63	51	147	24	7	.219/.319/.469	81	0.7
Russell Martin	C	LAN	MLB	36	249	29	5	0	6	20	30	60	1	0	.220/.337/.330	85	1.2
Zach McKinstry	SS	OKL	AAA	24	95	17	8	2	7	26	6	18	0	1	.382/.421/.753	152	1.0
	SS	TUL	AA	24	384	53	16	4	12	52	37	74	8	8	.279/.352/.455	147	2.7
Kristopher Negron	UT	LAN	MLB	33	57	9	1	0	2	7	3	17	0	1	.259/.298/.389	68	-0.4
	UT	TAC	AAA	33	356	62	15	4	12	61	41	91	11	3	.310/.396/.503	109	2.1
	UT	SEA	MLB	33	25	3	0	0	0	1	2	9	1	0	.217/.280/.217	77	0.0
Andy Pages	OF	OGD	Rk+	18	279	57	22	2	19	55	26	79	7	6	.298/.398/.651	173	2.6
Cristian Santana	3B	TUL	AA	22	413	45	22	1	10	57	10	88	0	0	.301/.320/.436	96	0.5
Tyler White	1B	LAN	MLB	28	26	2	0	0	0	2	4	4	0	0	.045/.192/.045	-11	-0.4
	1B	HOU	MLB	28	253	16	14	0	3	21	32	74	0	0	.225/.320/.330	86	-0.5

On December 31, 2019, **Jacob Amaya** tweeted "showers w the light off be hitting different !" Hitting different at High-A Rancho Cucamonga could double as a New Year's Resolution for the middle infield prospect, who struggled upon a late-season promotion. ⓘ A once-promising athletic catcher, **Austin Barnes** walked a lot and framed exceptionally well, but has now been reduced to the note that he had a 69 OPS+ over the last two seasons before he singled in his final at-bat of 2019 to bump it up to 70. Not-so-nice. ⓘ Signed for $6 million in 2015, Cuban-import **Omar Estevez** was billed as a pure hitter with questionable pop. While that evaluation has proved true, expectations were set a bit higher when he signed, making him yet another disappointing Estevez when it comes to sheen. ⓘ **Jedd Gyorko** put up a .416 OPS as a Dodger belying his true contribution to the team: a 'Jerk-Store' Dodgers jersey during Players' Weekend. ⓘ **Jeren Kendall**'s potential upside was the reason for his first-round selection and continues to be the carrot on the stick that the Dodgers desperately chase, but those Boston Dynamics robots are less mechanical than his swing. ⓘ A reunion with the team he began his career with didn't end in fairy tale fashion for **Russell Martin**, though that's likely because the Dodgers didn't use his prowess on the mound—now the all-time MLB ERA leader (minimum four innings)—in the playoffs. For shame. ⑫ A defensive maestro, **Zach McKinstry** orchestrated a virtuoso offensive performance in a 26-game sample at Triple-A, earning himself a standing ovation—and a spot on the 40-man roster. ⑫ The self-proclaimed "Negrón James" put up dominance worthy of the moniker in his first week after being acquired by the Dodgers with a 1.069 OPS. He then regressed to being **Kristopher Negrón** with a .354 OPS the rest of the way. ⑫ Signed out of Cuba for $300,000 in the 2018 international free agent period, **Andy Pages** gives the Dodgers a bat-first, high-OBP outfield prospect, and more pages than George R. R. Martin. ⑫ First, the good news: Since graduating from rookie ball, **Cristian Santana** has homered four more times than he's walked. Now, the bad news: He's walked four fewer times than he's homered. ⑫ Acquired for a literal (Andre) Scrubb, **Tyler White** quickly proved why his job security in Houston evaporated, going an almost impressive 1-for-22 with the Dodgers before hitting the 60-day IL with a trapezius strain.

Pitchers

PITCHER	TEAM	LVL	AGE	W	L	SV	G	GS	IP	H	HR	BB/9	K/9	K	GB%	WHIP	ERA	DRA	WARP
Pedro Baez	LAN	MLB	31	7	2	1	71	0	69²	43	6	3.0	8.9	69	37%	0.95	3.10	3.68	1.3
JT Chargois	OKL	AAA	28	1	2	4	27	0	32²	27	3	4.4	10.2	37	59%	1.32	2.76	2.53	1.2
	LAN	MLB	28	1	0	0	21	0	21¹	21	4	2.1	11.8	28	47%	1.22	6.33	3.66	0.4
Brett De Geus	GRL	A	21	4	2	4	19	0	30²	17	0	1.8	10.6	36	49%	0.75	2.35	2.22	0.9
	RCU	A+	21	2	0	4	20	0	31	28	0	2.0	10.5	36	65%	1.13	1.16	3.23	0.5
Victor Gonzalez	RCU	A+	23	2	1	0	8	5	27¹	17	0	4.6	11.9	36	52%	1.13	1.65	2.96	0.6
	TUL	AA	23	3	1	2	15	8	48¹	48	4	2.6	8.2	44	54%	1.28	2.23	4.59	0.2
	OKL	AAA	23	0	0	0	15	0	14	16	3	2.6	8.4	13	55%	1.43	3.86	4.83	0.2
Melvin Jimenez	OGD	Rk+	19	5	0	0	10	1	20	8	0	2.7	19.4	43	27%	0.70	2.25	1.40	0.9
	RCU	A+	19	2	0	2	19	0	30²	24	5	5.6	13.5	46	35%	1.40	3.52	3.70	0.4
Marshall Kasowski	TUL	AA	24	4	3	2	27	0	29¹	17	1	4.9	14.1	46	43%	1.12	2.45	3.13	0.5
Kevin Quackenbush	OKL	AAA	30	2	5	11	54	0	58²	59	9	2.5	13.0	85	37%	1.28	5.06	3.07	1.8
Edubray Ramos	LEH	AAA	26	2	0	6	10	0	10	6	1	3.6	7.2	8	36%	1.00	1.80	3.77	0.2
	PHI	MLB	26	1	0	0	20	0	15	19	5	4.2	6.6	11	28%	1.73	5.40	5.61	0.0
Casey Sadler	OKL	AAA	28	0	0	1	2	1	6	8	1	1.5	13.5	9	56%	1.50	6.00	2.03	0.3
	DUR	AAA	28	1	1	1	11	3	32²	30	5	1.4	12.1	44	40%	1.07	2.76	2.92	1.1
	TBA	MLB	28	0	0	0	9	0	19¹	16	2	2.3	5.1	11	55%	1.09	1.86	5.35	0.0
	LAN	MLB	28	4	0	1	24	1	27	25	3	2.7	6.7	20	52%	1.22	2.33	4.96	0.1
Edwin Uceta	RCU	A+	21	4	0	0	10	10	50¹	47	6	2.9	11.6	65	36%	1.25	2.15	3.72	0.8
	TUL	AA	21	7	2	0	16	14	73	62	5	4.1	9.4	76	44%	1.30	3.21	4.93	0.0

Three years ago, **Yadier Álvarez** was a consensus Top 50 prospect with a Zeusian arm. Now he's coming off a year in which he threw just a handful of innings due to injuries and a suspension for disciplinary issues, that make it seem like he's using that arm to throw his career away. ⑫ **Pedro Báez** is an above-average reliever who is frequently miscast as a great reliever to be used in key moments, which leads to predictably mixed results. ⚾ On a scale of 1-10, **JT Chargois'** handsomeness is probably about a 9. Unfortunately, he seems to believe the higher the number the better applies to ERA as well. ⚾ A transition to the bullpen came with a huge strikeout boost for **Brett de Geus**, which bodes well for his future as a high-leverage reliever as well as the opportunities for De Geus Ex Machina jokes for his bases loaded, no-out appearances. ⚾ Though he hasn't tossed a pitch above Triple-A, **Victor Gonzalez** could soon be joining Randy Choate, Adam Kolarek and Boone Logan in the anti-LOOGY class action lawsuit after having his big-prospects potentially diminished despite leaving a trail of left-handed hitters in his wake. ⚾ Right-hander **Melvin Jimenez** has a fairly classic scouting profile in that he misses lots of bats, allows too many walks, coughs up too many homers and probably used to go by "B.J." ⚾ **Marshall Kasowski** misses a ton of bats with a fastball that touches the upper 90s with ride and deception. Everything else, including his control, is iffy. ⚾ Named for the sound a duck makes after falling into shrubbery, **Kevin Quackenbush** also has trouble escaping jams; that's part of why he spent the whole year in Triple-A despite a flashy strikeout rate. ⚾ It was another injury-riddled campaign for **Edubray Ramos**, who missed significant chunks of time with shoulder injuries and lost nearly two miles an hour off both his fastball and slider when he was healthy enough to trudge to the mound in relief. ⚾ Let us hope that teenage righty pitching prospect **Jerming Rosario** never finds himself in the employ of one Joe Girardi, lest he forever become known as "Jermy." ⚾ Acquired midseason from Tampa Bay, **Casey Sadler** earned the Dodgers' 2019 Sword of Damocles award, as his shiny surface stats (ERA) outpaced his concerning peripherals (FIP, DRA) and fans waited for disaster to strike with every outing. ⚾ Striking out over a batter per inning is good. Also good, **Edwin Uceta**'s name anagrams perfectly to CA We United, which, you know, really provides some extra juice to endear the righty to his future west coast fanbase.

Dodgers Prospects

The State of the System
The Dodgers system is shallower and more top-heavy than the last few years, but still has a lot of impact, major-league-ready talent ready for a win-now club.

The Top Ten

———— ★ ★ ★ *2020 Top 101 Prospect* **#3** ★ ★ ★ ————

1 **Gavin Lux SS**   OFP: 70   ETA: 2019
Born: 11/23/97   Age: 22   Bats: L   Throws: R   Height: 6'2"   Weight: 190
Origin: Round 1, 2016 Draft (#20 overall)

The Report: I've written a lot about Lux this year, and the tl;dr version is that sometimes you see a player and you know. Lux showed an elite approach at a young age in Double-A, with advanced pitch recognition that heralded his ability to translate a quality hit tool to the highest level. It's a legitimate shortstop profile, and when you see that play with flashes of plus power in games, it's a special sight. Lux continued to impress around the diamond as his athleticism, body control, and instincts manifested themselves in all facets of his game on through the high minors to ultimately force a big-league promotion at 21.

He generates plus bat speed with the ability to get his bat to the ball with strength and quickness anywhere in the zone. Lux attacks the meat of the zone aggressively while remaining patient on pitchers' pitches early in the count. He's happy to take a free pass, and his selectiveness allows him to tap into his plus power to launch the ball out of the park. He also is adept at going with a pitch to drive the ball to left-center. To round out the profile, Lux is a plus runner, and while he hasn't shown as an especially efficient base-stealer, his excellent instincts and speed allow him to add baserunning value in other ways.

As of now Lux fits well at shortstop, where his clean hands, plus reactions and lateral range make up for an average arm. He plays with an aggressive, high-effort style rather than smooth, natural grace, and he may have to move off the position down the line on account of a frame that should continue to add bulk as he ages. Lux can play as an average shortstop until then, or slide over to the keystone with above-average defense.

When you put the package together, you have yourself one of the best prospects in baseball. Lux should be a plus regular at the major league level, and there's a relatively high chance (as these things go) he's an impact player and All-Star.

Variance: Low. There is a decent chance he fills out and needs to move to second or third on the sooner side of later. But the bat should provide impact value at any infield position, so long as the pitch recognition carries over to the majors.

Ben Carsley's Fantasy Take: Few players offer a better combination of floor and upside than Lux, who will seemingly "bottom out" as a top-12 third baseman but who's got a shot to place as a top-10 second basemen or shortstop as well. Even a modest projection for Lux sees him as a four-category fantasy contributor, and I still think his speed and athleticism could eventually translate to 10-plus steals a year as well. History has proven time and time again that there's no such thing as a truly "safe" prospect, but given Lux's well-roundedness, ETA, and organization, he's about as close to safe as we can possibly hope for.

★ ★ ★ *2020 Top 101 Prospect* **#8** ★ ★ ★

2 Dustin May   RHP   OFP: 70   ETA: 2019
Born: 09/06/97 Age: 22 Bats: R Throws: R Height: 6'6" Weight: 180
Origin: Round 3, 2016 Draft (#101 overall)

The Report: The lanky redhead's rise to the big leagues has been well documented here at BP, and he is a great example of a player who is unorthodox and well represents the value of eyes-on scouting.

May brings a big fastball to the party. He'll sit mid 90s with it, and he was topping out in triple digits out of LA's pen down the stretch last year. He pairs it with a devastating curveball that spins like a top, though he'll lack consistency with the pitch's shape. Also in the arsenal is a hard slider-ish cutter in the low 90s, and every now and again he'll turn over a changeup in the low 80s that can fool hitters with its movement. The stuff itself is electric, and while the command could unsurprisingly stand to improve, he actually controls his frame quite effectively.

Despite being 6-foot-6, May's mechanics aren't awkward like you might expect; he works out of a three-quarters slot with a smooth arm action and release, and those Go-Go Gadget limbs help give him quality extension towards the plate. There's some room for May to gain additional muscle, though it's unlikely to be the bulky kind.

Variance: Low. There are things May needs to work on, the command first and foremost, but even if he never maxes out on that front the stuff is such that he'll be a valuable pitcher in the big leagues barring calamity.

Ben Carsley's Fantasy Take: As good as May is, he lacks the truly elite strikeout upside that fantasy's true No. 1 starters need. Thus concludes the negative things we can say about Dustin May: Dynasty Prospect. He's already reached the majors. He's got favorable contextual factors. He misses bats, he won't kill your WHIP, and he should earn a ton of wins on the Dodgers unless they get weird with their usage. They get there in very different ways, but from a pure output standpoint, he could end up being a similar fantasy asset to Aaron Nola. History has proven time and time again that there's no such thing as a truly "safe" pitching prospect, but given May's well-roundedness, ETA, and organization, he's about as close to safe as we can possibly hope for.

★ ★ ★ *2020 Top 101 Prospect* **#61** ★ ★ ★

3 **Josiah Gray   RHP**   OFP: 60   ETA: 2021
Born: 12/21/97   Age: 22   Bats: R   Throws: R   Height: 6'1"   Weight: 190
Origin: Round 2, 2018 Draft (#72 overall)

The Report: The Cincinnati Reds selected Gray with the 72nd-overall pick of the 2018 draft, then promptly shipped him to Los Angeles as part of the Yasiel Puig trade several months later. In his first season in the Dodgers' system, the right-hander excelled across three levels and was named the organization's Minor League Pitcher of the Year. A former college shortstop turned hurler, he proved durable in 2019, throwing 130 combined innings across his three stops. Gray attacks the strike zone with no-nonsense efficiency and plus command of a heavy, mid-90s fastball. He sets the tone with that pitch getting ahead with it, or generating quick outs. A tight slider that can sit as high as 85 plays well off of the heater, and a developing mid-to-upper-80s changeup rounds out what projects as a solid three-pitch mix. Although none of his pitches grade out better than plus, Gray's confidence to attack with all of them keeps pressure on opposing hitters. He's a competitor on the mound, with a good work ethic and live arm that combine to set a high floor.

Variance: Medium. The secondaries are still work-in-progress stage, with room for improved command and consistency.

Ben Carsley's Fantasy Take: On the one hand, the Dodgers are about as good an organization as a pitching prospect can ask to be in; their track record with recent prospects speaks for itself, and they offer a favorable home ballpark and good supporting team upon reaching the majors. On the other hand, the Dodgers have a lot of pitching talent right now, and Gray lacks the upside needed to assure himself of a full-time spot in the rotation. Thus, we're presented with a quandary: is it better if Gray sticks with the Dodgers and reaps the organizational benefits, or is it better if he gets shipped to an org in which he'd have a clearer path to start? Either way, if your dynasty league rosters 100 prospects, you should be willing to burn a roster spot to find out.

Los Angeles Dodgers 2020

──────── ★ ★ ★ *2020 Top 101 Prospect* **#65** ★ ★ ★ ────────

4 **Miguel Vargas   3B**   OFP: 60   ETA: 2021
Born: 11/17/99   Age: 20   Bats: R   Throws: R   Height: 6'3"   Weight: 205
Origin: International Free Agent, 2017

The Report: Signed by the Dodgers after defecting with his father in 2017, the now-20-year-old Cuban infielder impressed as a wee 19-year-old across two levels of A-ball. He plays a savvy defensive third base, displaying soft hands, a strong throwing arm, and impressive mobility and body control. At 6-foot-3 and 205 pounds, Vargas shows quality athleticism in a frame that is in the process of getting stronger. The raw power is growing right along with him. His exceptional hand-eye coordination, bat-to-ball ability, and professional gap-to-gap hitting approach stand out; his at-bats have a plan, and he executes a quality swing when he gets his pitch. He's surprisingly fleet of foot at present, keenly cutting the basepaths with solid acceleration. It was a season of exciting growth for Vargas, and he ends it as the biggest mover in the system.

Variance: High. He's talented, but he's young, and he's on an aggressive trajectory.

Ben Carsley's Fantasy Take: The time to get in on Vargas in most dynasty leagues has come and gone, but if you play in a shallower setting you might still be able to capitalize on his relative lack of fantasy buzz. Vargas' ceiling isn't sky-high, but at the end of the day, is he really that different from Ke'Bryan Hayes? I don't think he is, yet Hayes seems to have a lot more name value at this point. That should change.

──────── ★ ★ ★ *2020 Top 101 Prospect* **#79** ★ ★ ★ ────────

5 **Keibert Ruiz   C**   OFP: 55   ETA: 2022
Born: 07/20/98   Age: 21   Bats: B   Throws: R   Height: 6'0"   Weight: 200
Origin: International Free Agent, 2015

The Report: After breaking out across two levels in 2017 then holding his own as a 19-year-old in Double-A in 2018, Ruiz nearly cracked the top 30 of last winter's 101. 2019 saw the backstop take a couple steps back, however. Ruiz is a bat-first catcher whose best tool is his ability to make contact from both sides, and we've had evaluators put a comfortable 6 on the hit. The approach has stagnated, however, and one of Ruiz's flaws has been an inability to develop enough selectivity at the plate. His free-swinging tendencies are mitigated some by the superior bat-to-ball skill, but he hasn't yet been able to optimize his contact against higher-end pitching. To that end, the power has also revealed as a bit of a concern; he'll show average raw with flashes of in-game, but the right-handed swing in particular is flatter and lacks explosiveness through the ball at present.

Behind the plate, Ruiz still remains a work in progress. His ability to smother balls and handle things around the plate is notable, as is a firm glove hand on receipt. But he has struggled on plays that require him to come out of the crouch and move laterally. Some of those struggles are simply the product of his general lack of experience—bear in mind he is still just 21—but the frame is also on the bulkier side, and the body thickened up by a few more pounds this season. Ruiz's arm is a solid-average tool, and he has the raw tools he needs to stay behind the plate; it's all about refinement in both ability and physique.

Variance: High. This is less about the risk Ruiz carries and more about the ceiling. If Ruiz becomes more selective at the plate, matures his body to develop more power and athleticism while cleaning up his issues on defense he's an above-average major league catcher. He's young enough, and he has advanced quickly enough, that there remains an expectation that he can make these adjustments.

Ben Carsley's Fantasy Take: Ruiz was my test case. After years of "missing" (or at least not being able to accept the opportunity cost associated with rostering) on guys like Blake Swihart, Francisco Mejia, Chance Sisco, et al., Ruiz was where I decided to draw the line. I'm out on catching prospects for dynasty now, even when they're as promising with the bat as Ruiz is. The lead times are too unpredictable, the developmental hurdles too numerous, the gaps between MLB ETA and fantasy ETA too wide. Ruiz is a fun prospect, and I fully respect those who'll choose to dive in on him; they may be rewarded with a Willson Contreras-esque fantasy asset. To me, that upside isn't worth the risk.

★ ★ ★ *2020 Top 101 Prospect* **#81** ★ ★ ★

6 Tony Gonsolin   RHP   OFP: 55   ETA: 2019
Born: 05/14/94   Age: 26   Bats: R   Throws: R   Height: 6'3"   Weight: 205
Origin: Round 9, 2016 Draft (#281 overall)

The Report: A former ninth-round senior sign back when he threw 89-90, Gonsolin has just kept right on keepin' on as a professional, ultimately battling his way through 40 successful debut innings in Los Angeles last year after surviving the Triple-A moon ball. His four pitches all play up off each other, starting with a fastball that nowadays will sit 93-95 and tickle 96. There isn't a ton of movement or explosiveness to it, but a nasty trap-door splitter tunnels really well off its line, and there's deception in his slow-building delivery to add some sneaky perceived velocity to the heater. A noted cat lover, he can miss bats with two distinct spinners, and has shown an aptitude for carving off weak fly-ball contact with both of those offerings. He's a good athlete who shows fluidity and solid balance in his delivery, though there's some herk-and-jerk and stab to his arm action that continues to wobble the command. First-look deception and pitchability helped him get away with some looseness around the zone in his debut, but free passes and wandering fastballs will threaten his peripherals and pose the biggest threat to his ceiling as an above-average member of a first-division staff.

Variance: Low. He's big league-ready, and already showed he could hang with the big boys last year.

Ben Carsley's Fantasy Take: Take all the concerns we mentioned with Gray, now dial down the upside even more. Gonsolin might make for an acceptable spot starter/depth guy if you're competing in 2020, but otherwise you should be aiming for profiles with more impact potential.

7. Diego Cartaya C OFP: 60 ETA: 2023
Born: 09/07/01 Age: 18 Bats: R Throws: R Height: 6'2" Weight: 199
Origin: International Free Agent, 2018

The Report: One of the top international prospects in the 2018 class, Cartaya showed well enough in his professional debut in the Dominican that the notoriously-aggressive Los Angeles front office brought him stateside as a 17-year-old. He's got a thick, mature frame, but there's exciting baseline athleticism. Cartaya already moves well behind the dish, and there's an overall physicality that's fun to dream on. His hands are a little stiff right now, but they're quick, strong, and accurate to the ball, and there's cause for cautious optimism that he can develop into a solid receiver. The swing is already very pretty; he'll drift into the zone a bit, but he takes fluid, strong rips from the right side, and could grow into above-average power. Everything's to the pull-side right now, but he sees pitches well and puts good wood on the ball. He is obviously eons away from being anywhere close to a finished product, but the early returns on the club's substantial investment are good, and it should surprise nobody if he finds his way to Great Lakes next season.

Variance: Extreme. The range of outcomes is as enormous as the timeline for him to actualize his exciting starter's set of tools. Catcher development is frequently disjointed and weird, even in organizations with strong recent track records of developing the position.

Ben Carsley's Fantasy Take: If I'm not super in on Ruiz, you can imagine how I feel about Cartaya. If you opt to invest in dynasty catching prospects, more power to you. I'll be using my roster spots differently.

8. Jeter Downs SS OFP: 55 ETA: 2021
Born: 07/27/98 Age: 21 Bats: R Throws: R Height: 5'11" Weight: 180
Origin: Round 1, 2017 Draft (#32 overall)

The Report: The second prospect coming back to the sunshine state for Yasiel Puig last winter, Downs showed a solid power-and-speed combination from the shortstop position in his age-20 season. He led the California League with 33 doubles, then continued to rake during a cameo at Double-A, tying off his season with a three-homer game in the Texas League playoffs. After a pull-happy first half, Downs made adjustments to better utilize the opposite field in the second half, and both the hit and game power tools flourished. There isn't really a carrying tool in the offensive toolbag; he's got a decent approach and there's solid-average pop, but he stills cuts off the outer half too often. He's an above-average runner whose instincts play amplify his baserunning skill and should allow him to continue stealing bases at a solid clip. Defensively, the athletic 5-foot-10 middle infielder has good mobility and receptive hands, along with a 50-grade arm that is reasonable enough to cut it at the six, if not ideal for the role. It's more comfortable as a second base projection, but he should be able to stay up the middle and add occasional shortstop utility. The bat will lead him to the big leagues, however, and while the Dodgers' depth may delay Downs' debut, he should be scratching at the major league door by 2021.

Variance: Medium-to-High. The bat-to-ball consistency will dictate whether he's a toolsy bench asset or an everyday contributor.

Ben Carsley's Fantasy Take: Downs might actually be a better dynasty prospect than an IRL one thanks to his power and speed combo. That being said, I'm lower on him than some of my dynasty-loving colleagues, as I think he has utility infielder written all over him if he stays in this org. Downs is more interesting than most players with this profile because of the potential for modest contributions in every category but average. Even so, the upside remains fairly modest.

9. Kody Hoese 3B OFP: 50 ETA: 2021
Born: 07/13/97 Age: 22 Bats: R Throws: R Height: 6'4" Weight: 200
Origin: Round 1, 2019 Draft (#25 overall)

The Report: The first of the Dodgers' two first-rounders last summer, Hoese is a big, strong kid who pounded the ball during his junior season at Tulane and then kept right on hitting after signing. The stance is rigid and muscley, but he's a fluid mover whose strength translates into a quick burst at first move. He'll drift deep and lengthen his leveraged swing, so there's swing-and-miss risk here that can threaten the utility of his plus raw power. He's a patient hitter, however, and he showed an encouraging ability to stay in the zone in his debut. A sore elbow limited him defensively down the stretch, and there is some variance in the early defensive reports, with some seeing an instinctual player who will provide value at the hot corner, while others see a stiffer, fringe-averagier contributor with more limited range.

Variance: High. He'll give us more of a clue about how his later-popping college bat will translate to pro pitching next year.

Ben Carsley's Fantasy Take: Honestly, it's been like two years since Max Muncy and they're already gonna move forward with a remake?

10. Gerardo Carrillo RHP OFP: 50 ETA: 2021
Born: 09/13/98 Age: 21 Bats: R Throws: R Height: 5'10" Weight: 154
Origin: International Free Agent, 2016

The Report: Carrillo spent all of this season in the California League as a slight 20-year-old, but while the placement may have been a bit aggressive, he threw well enough at Great Lakes in 2018 to make it a reasonable challenge. He didn't fare well production-wise, pitching to a 5.22 DRA while walking 51 across 86 innings, but he showed plenty of raw material to get excited about.

He's not a big guy, at all, but the carrying tool is effortless mid-90s gas that ran up to 98 during the season and wandered into triple digits during his stint in the Arizona Fall League. The pitch features some run and sink, allowing him to get under barrels and generate plenty of ground-ball contact. A curve in the 78-82 band breaks with big—though early—vertical action. He sells the pitch well, but it does hump enough for some of the better hitters in the league to identify and lay off. His third pitch is a mid-80s slider that remains in the developmental stage; he's still trying to get a feel for it, but it tunnels well with the fastball, and has the chance to develop into an average pitch down the line. There is a changeup, but it's a distant fourth pitch with modest action.

He missed time with a shoulder injury that didn't sound great at the time, but he looked healthy and strong in the fall. There is enough athleticism, youth, and room for improvement in the mechanics to project some growth for his underwhelming present command, and he can grow into a devastating double-plus fastball with an above-average breaking ball.

Variance: Very High, bordering on extreme. His impressive showing in the AFL gave a glimpse of his potential if and when healthy, but here's a significant developmental road still ahead.

Ben Carsley's Fantasy Take: t's hard to imagine he's anything other than a reliever in this system. Pass.

The Next Ten

11. Michael Busch   2B
Born: 11/09/97   Age: 22   Bats: L   Throws: R   Height: 6'0"   Weight: 207
Origin: Round 1, 2019 Draft (#31 overall)

The Dodgers' other first-rounder last summer (compensation for not signing J.T. Ginn in 2018), Busch is a thick, athletic left-handed college bat with a solid offensive pedigree. It's a pretty swing with nice balance and loft, and while the bat speed doesn't stand out, he's strong and carves a tight path to the ball. He's also a disciplined hitter, with quality pitch recognition and the willingness and ability to drive pitches to the opposite field. It looks the part of eventually-above-average hit and game power tools. The defensive future is less clear; he played a bunch of first base and outfield as an amateur, and there's some lumber to the stride that suggests a future home at the former. The Dodgers are unconvinced, however, as they shifted him over to the keystone after he signed. The early returns on that experiment didn't look great, though some leeway is warranted given the newness of it all. He crammed in a couple games at Great Lakes down the stretch, and that'll be his likely landing spot to start 2020.

12 DJ Peters OF
Born: 12/12/95 Age: 24 Bats: R Throws: R Height: 6'6" Weight: 225
Origin: Round 4, 2016 Draft (#131 overall)

At 6-foot-6 and 235 pounds Peters has the ideal build for a power forward, or perhaps a Greek god if you're feeling classical. He's on the large side for a baseball player, and the athleticism took a small step back last year, though he's still a very good athlete with the ability to control his body and generate quick-twitchy movements.

At the plate this physicality translates to plus bat speed and the ability to find the barrel for tremendous exit velocities when he makes contact. It's plus-plus raw power, which is a good starting point, but he has extremely long levers and despite the speed of his barrel acceleration he'll struggle to catch up to premium velocity. He has also consistently struggled to recognize breaking balls and offspeed, and significant strikeout issues cap the hit tool and take a bite out of the in-game power. On the bright side, Peters has maintained a quality approach into the high minors, off-setting his whiffs with strong walk rates.

He's shown the ability to hang as a fringy centerfielder and may retain some utility there in the early years of his major league career, but he's a better fit as a potentially above-average defender in one of the corners. He's got the tools and talent to add value as a fourth outfielder, and if enough of the power plays the profile will carry him to an major league regular spot.

13 Jacob Amaya IF
Born: 09/03/98 Age: 21 Bats: R Throws: R Height: 6'0" Weight: 180
Origin: Round 11, 2017 Draft (#340 overall)

Amaya is just a fundamentally solid ball player. The feel and instincts for the infield are impeccable; his hands are silky smooth, and he consistently makes firm, accurate throws. He might not have the high-end quickness you want to see from a shortstop, but he makes up for it with sound execution and there's a broad enough defensive skill set that he can add value all over the dirt. At the plate, he has a modest leg kick, and uses it well to generate solid bat speed. There are elements of a solid hitter here, starting with an excellent approach that keeps him in the zone and in solid hitting counts, and the pop is sneaky to the gaps. There's a bit of tweener risk here, but he plays well above his tools and he finds enough ways to positively impact the game that he can grow into a valuable member of someone's 25-man roster in the next couple years.

14 Omar Estevez   IF
Born: 02/25/98   Age: 22   Bats: R   Throws: R   Height: 5'10"   Weight: 185
Origin: International Free Agent, 2015

Estevez has never lacked for a notable swing, and the hit tool took another cautious step forward last year at Double-A before he ran out of gas in the AFL. Nothing's changed a ton about the profile. The swing's unconventional, with an early hip turn that helps him put some juice into it and create some loft to the pull side. He's aggressive in the zone, but he does a decent job recognizing spin and offspeed, and he should get to the fringe-average power in games. His whiff and walk rates both went the right way last year, but he'll show vulnerability away, and pitchers may exploit it going forward. He split time between short and second again, though he played almost exclusively the latter in the second half. He's better-suited to the keystone, where his average arm can play and he can better cover his inconsistent reactions. He's still very young, and while his development to date has jerked and halted, he's made encouraging progress on a relatively short timeline. There's no carrying tool here, but he can be a nice middle-of-the-infield player to have around.

15 Mitchell White   RHP
Born: 12/28/94   Age: 25   Bats: R   Throws: R   Height: 6'3"   Weight: 210
Origin: Round 2, 2016 Draft (#65 overall)

You tell me you've got an idea of what Mitchell White turns into at this point, and I'll tell you yer a dang liar. It was another in an increasingly long line of injury-interrupted, inconsistent seasons for the now-24-year-old. While he managed to avoid any major maladies, he found the injured list on three separate occasions over the course of a season that saw him dominate Double-A (third time's a charm) before running headlong into the Triple-A ball. Despite a good dose of athleticism, White's never been able to key in on consistent mechanics, and his velocity will fluctuate pretty significantly from start to start. He actually pitched pretty well in the majority of his 16 PCL appearances last season, but his clunkers—including a gruesome 11-run start in August—underscore the volatility of his stuff on any given day. A low-90s cutter and downer curveball both show above-average potential, with the latter laying claim among the system's best when it's on. The durability concerns are significant, as are questions as to whether he'll ever develop something to round out an arsenal that once again got rolled pretty hard by left-handed hitters. Assuming he's physically able, he should enter the mix for big-league innings at some point next year, and how it all turns out from here…well, we'll all learn together.

16 Connor Wong   C
Born: 05/19/96   Age: 24   Bats: R   Throws: R   Height: 6'1"   Weight: 181
Origin: Round 3, 2017 Draft (#100 overall)

Wong has interesting physical and defensive profiles that offset some severe flaws enough to make him a fun wildcard in the system. The right/right catcher is 23 and just finished terrorizing Double-A in a short 40-game stint after spending the better part of two seasons at High-A.

Wong has excellent coordination that allows him to make hard line drive contact consistently, but the combination of an extreme arm bar, aggressive approach, and trouble recognizing breaking balls lead to outlandishly high strikeout rates that threaten to derail the offensive profile. The arm bar helps him generate power, but it also creates huge holes up and on the inner third. He's athletic enough to bet on an ability to integrate mechanical changes, but there's work ahead.

Defensively, Wong has solid hands behind the plate, and while he doesn't always have a smooth path to the ball, he performs well enough vertically and on the edges of the zone to add some value with his receiving. He has good footwork on blocks and a quick transition out of the crouch, which helps an average arm to play. The organization has flirted with second- and third-base reps for him, as well.

Wong currently projects to a tandem catching role at the major league level if he can shorten up the upper half of his swing and continue to bring his pop into games against experienced arms.

17 Michael Grove   RHP
Born: 12/18/96   Age: 23   Bats: R   Throws: R   Height: 6'3"   Weight: 200
Origin: Round 2, 2018 Draft (#68 overall)

After recovering from Tommy John surgery, the club's second-rounder in 2018 eased into his professional debut with 51 2/3 very interesting innings in the California League. He got pummeled by terrible luck on batted balls all year, but the progress of his stuff is the real story. Grove is lean, strong, and extremely athletic, with good body control that should allow him to repeat a clean delivery, though his deep drop onto his backside caused timing issues as he knocked off rust all year. He comes from a high, over-the-top slot that gives his tight breaker a bunch of vertical action. The fastball sits 91-93, topping at 95, and while it doesn't feature tremendous life, it spins hard and he locates it to both sides of the plate with two-way movement. Grove doesn't presently have a plus pitch, but you can tell there is plenty of confidence in what he does have, and given the physicality it shouldn't surprise anyone if the velocity takes another step forward and pushes the heater into plus range assuming improved command. He's a prime candidate to move up this list with another healthy season in Double-A next year.

18 Dennis Santana   RHP
Born: 04/12/96   Age: 24   Bats: R   Throws: R   Height: 6'2"   Weight: 190
Origin: International Free Agent, 2013

A year ago Santana capped a storybook rise with a major league debut, but then he hurt his rotator cuff and never looked quite all the way back to form in 2019. The fastball dropped a couple ticks, and he couldn't find the handle on its still-well-above-average movement. The poor command and diminished velocity proved a dangerous combination with the Triple-A ball, and he got absolutely pummeled in 17 starts to the tune of a ghastly 8.00 ERA. That precipitated a perhaps inevitable transition to the bullpen, where he settled things down a bit in spite of ongoing control issues. The club has worked hard to streamline what was once a significant crossfire, but he has struggled to sync up his timing and attack the zone consistently, even as he has continued to miss bats at a solid clip. At its best his four-seamer moves an obscene amount and pairs with a slider that flashes above-average and works effectively as a chase pitch, and the hope is that as he gets farther away from the shoulder issue he'll get back on track and into the mix for important relief innings in LA in 2020.

19 Cristian Santana   3B/1B
Born: 02/24/97   Age: 23   Bats: R   Throws: R   Height: 6'2"   Weight: 175
Origin: International Free Agent, 2014

Signed by the Dodgers in 2014 out of the Dominican Republic, the 22-year-old third baseman ranked third in the Texas League with a .301 batting average last season while improving his strikeout rate in spite of the difficult jump to Double-A. He's done a lot of work to tone down some seriously wild-swinging ways, but even as he now stays in better control of his ferocious hacks, he has remained an extremely aggressive hitter. It's really not a profile that typically yields confidence in the bat holding up, though Santana has defied the odds to this point. The former shortstop has good mobility and receptive hands when guarding the corners, and it's more likely today than it was at this time last year that he'll be able to stick at third (at least most of the time). His strong throwing arm is well-suited for the hot corner, and he can compensate for the occasional lapse in technique with plus raw arm strength. The good outcome here is an Adam Jones freak who hangs on to play a passable D on the left side, and there's cult favorite potential if that happens on account of a dynamic Puig-like electricity to his game.

20 Brett de Geus   RHP
Born: 11/04/97   Age: 22   Bats: R   Throws: R   Height: 6'2"   Weight: 190
Origin: Round 33, 2017 Draft (#1000 overall)

Drafted by the Dodgers out of Cabrillo Community College in the 33rd-round of the 2017 draft (the 1000th overall selection!), de Geus had a breakout season in 2019 after transitioning from starting to relief work. The 21-year-old held Midwest League hitters to a .163 average across 19 outings and didn't miss a beat after a promotion to the California League, where he struck out 36 batters with a 1.16 ERA in 20 appearances out of the bullpen. The 6-foot-2 righty aggressively attacks the strike-zone with a 94-96 mph sinking fastball, an 87-89 mph slider/cutter thing, and a hard-biting 81-83 mph curveball with 11-to-5 shape. His low three-quarters slot is efficient and repeatable, and his advanced command of three quality pitches could have him contributing to the big club's bullpen as soon as late-2020.

Personal Cheeseball

PC

Edwin Ríos 4C
Born: 04/21/94 Age: 26 Bats: L Throws: R Height: 6'3" Weight: 220
Origin: Round 6, 2015 Draft (#192 overall)

I've spun many a tantalizing yarn about Edwin Ríos' majestic power on these pages, and he didn't disappoint in his long-anticipated major league debut. It was a tiny, meaningless sample, but dude's exit velocity was up there in Judge/Sanó range in his limited looks at big-league pitching, and that's fun! Not much of anything has changed in his profile or projection; he is smooth and sure-handed in the field, but he's also slower than a spoon of molasses slathered onto a sloth's fur coat, and it's just not a realistic third-base future. That means he's gotta hit. And keep hitting. And then hit some more. And he's going to have to do that in spite of an approach that gets C.J. Cron a little flushed. He's made it work at just about every step along the way, which is why we continue to write about him. But it's a narrow, fraught path to generating enough positive value with the bat to justify a 26-man slot on a modern roster. The hope here, obviously, is that he does just that.

Low Minors Sleeper

LMS

Andy Pages OF
Born: 12/08/00 Age: 19 Bats: R Throws: R Height: 6'1" Weight: 180
Origin: International Free Agent, 2018

Pages was a late 2017-18 sign out of the Dominican, where he made a successful debut last year before migrating to Extended last spring and the Pioneer League last summer. And by gum, if you squinted and adjusted your old-man spectacles up and down just so, that right there was a young Justin Turner in the batter's box! Pages' frame is mature for a kid who just turned 19, and he channels his strength into a lofted swing with quality bat speed. The stance is vertical, the hands show signs of loading consistently off a large leg kick, and he explodes through the hitting zone. There isn't as much physical projection remaining as your typical teenager, but the raw power should grow into plus territory. He's struck out a good bit in his young career, but that's not necessarily surprising given the complex hitting mechanics, and it's consistently loud contact when he makes it. He's an entertaining, confident hitter in the box. He played center for the majority of his reps last summer in the Pioneer League, but it's a corner profile with heavier legs that produce average-at-best foot speed. Given the advanced offensive development he's likely to see full-season ball next year, and he'll be a fun one to monitor once he does.

Top Talents 25 and Under (as of 4/1/2020)

1. Cody Bellinger
2. Walker Buehler
3. Corey Seager
4. Gavin Lux
5. Dustin May
6. Will Smith
7. Julio Urias
8. Alex Verdugo
9. Josiah Gray
10. Miguel Vargas

The first two names on this list should come as a surprise to no one. Bellinger just authored an MVP season while spending time at first base in addition to fields center and right, and graded out to a cumulative +15 FRAA. His 158 DRC+ was second to only Christian Yelich (167) in the National League. Given that his greatest competition for the top spot on this list is a pitcher with Tommy John surgery on his resume, it wasn't a difficult call. That pitcher, Buehler, assumed the mantle of staff ace from Clayton Kershaw this year, even if he was statistically overshadowed by Hyun-Jin Ryu for much of it. There's no one Manager Dave Roberts and company trust more with the season on the line than the flamethrower with the coat-hanger frame. With good reason, too: Buehler produced a 2.89 DRA to go with his 215 strikeouts in 182 1/3 innings–good for 5.7 WARP, which ranked 7th in the National League and 11th in MLB.

The biggest pain point in this process was slotting in Seager. The Dodgers' current shortstop produced a three-win season, but much of that was based on solid fielding from a valuable position, given his mild 106 DRC+. Given how much positioning factors in to Seager's ability to man the position, it's fair to wonder how much credit is really his to claim. Seager has also produced two four-win seasons in recent memory, but injuries took away most of 2018 while striking just as his bat started to heat up a couple times in 2019. It's not unfair to prefer the shiny new option (Lux), but Seager topped our prospect list back in 2015, speaking to the upside present in a guy who has produced 13 wins already in his career. There's nothing to say Lux won't meet the same or similar obstacles as Seager has, even if recency bias has us wishcasting that he doesn't. Seager earns the spot here due to actually doing at the top level, but if you prefer the risk proposition that Lux offers, we won't blame you.

May vs. Smith offers a similarly intriguing argument, especially since the latter has "done it" in the majors a bit more than the former. Still, as good as Smith was overall, it's easy to use some admittedly arbitrary endpoints to call into question whether the league adjusted or he tired. He became the full-time catcher around July 27th. Over his first 19 games, Smith slashed .339/.411/.887. Over his next 26 games (until the end of the season), he nosedived down to .183/.277/.305. He ended the season with a .907 OPS and was solid, if not better, behind the dish. This ranking is a bet that he sees some offensive regression as he starts consistently over the course of a full season, though we're still quite high on the overall package he offers.

For his part, May flashed in his brief major-league stint. He recorded some solid overall surface stats that bely an uglier DRA (4.55) but shiny FIP (2.85). His stuff was tremendous, though, as his fastball demonstrated enough run that it could viably Beat the Freeze, and a useful cut fastball that tricked batters because they had to consider the running two-seamer. His vaunted curveball came and went, and it seems like the different grip/seams on the major-league (and Triple-A) ball might have played a part there. Slotting May in over Smith is a gamble that he figures that out and ascends to mid-rotation status while flashing more over the course of the next season.

Urias fails to join May above Smith only because it isn't at all clear how many innings he can muster. He accrued just shy of 80 in 2019, which doesn't exactly forebode a full season in the rotation. He also needs to demonstrate his progress as a human being after earning a 20-game suspension after he was arrested for suspicion of domestic violence, where witnesses allege he shoved his girlfriend to the ground in a parking lot.

Verdugo is a logical endpoint for the eligible major leaguers on this list. He started out quite hot, tailed off, and then missed most of August and all of September due to injury. He's limited to the corner outfield, so there is significant pressure on the bat to produce enough value to justify his playing time. That said, his (limited) success in the big leagues is enough to easily earn him a spot ahead of the third- and fourth-ranked prospects in the system.

Part 3: Featured Articles

The Baseball Is Juiced (Again)

Robert Arthur

This article originally appeared at Baseball Prospectus on April 5, 2019.

It started when the normally reliable Chris Sale got lit up for three homers by the Mariners in the Red Sox's season opener. It was part of a record number of taters that flew on Opening Day, as starters from Sale to Zack Greinke were taken deep by the handful. Then Christian Yelich hit a home run in each of his first four games, tying yet another MLB record, this one for consecutive games with a dinger to start a season.

It didn't take long for fans and players to begin whispering and tweeting about the baseballs being juiced again. It's early yet for us to come to any definitive conclusion about the 2019 season, but preliminary data shows that the baseball has returned to its aerodynamic peak. Whether that means this season will smash home run records like 2017 did remains to be seen.

Before home run explosion over the last few years, no one worried too much about the baseball's air resistance. While MLB and Rawlings (the company that manufactures the official baseballs) kept track of dozens of metrics to make sure that the ball was consistent from month to month, they didn't measure drag.

But drag is incredibly important in determining how likely a hitter is to knock one out of the park. As baseballs become more aerodynamic, they travel further given a certain initial velocity. A deep fly ball that might have been caught at the warning track can instead go into the first row of the stands. A three percent change in drag coefficient can work to add about five feet to a well-hit fly ball, which can in turn increase home runs league wide by an astounding 10-15 percent.

It's possible to measure the aerodynamics of the baseball using the pitch-tracking radars currently in place in each MLB ballpark. By calculating the loss of speed from when the pitch is released to when it crosses the plate, you can directly measure the drag coefficient on the baseball. I first wrote about the role of decreasing drag in boosting home runs in 2017, and MLB's commission of scientists and statisticians later confirmed that the more aerodynamic baseballs in use that year were largely to blame for the spike in home runs. The same commission rejected some alternate hypotheses, like rising temperatures and a league-wide boost in launch angle pushing more balls over the fence.

The current era has featured some large fluctuations in drag coefficient, leading to first an explosion in 2016 and 2017, and then a dialing back of homers last year. Curious about the record-breaking home run tallies in the last few days, I used the same methodology to measure the aerodynamics of the baseballs so far in 2019.

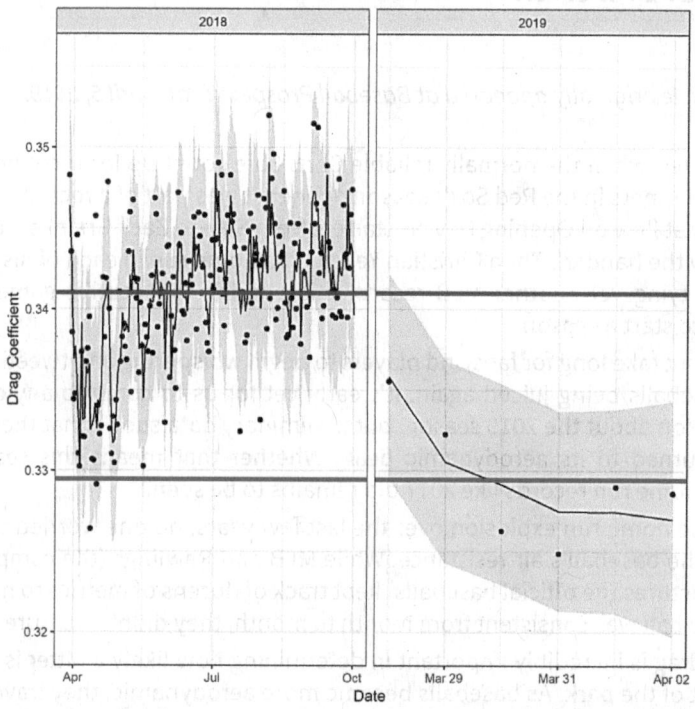

We're only a week into the 2019 season, but the drag numbers so far are among the lowest recorded in the last calendar year. With apologies for gory math, the current 2019 season average drag coefficient (the red line) would be below the 95 percent credible interval (the shaded area) for about nine-tenths of the 2018 season. (I used a Bayesian Random Walk model implemented in INLA to calculate these credible intervals, averaging the drag numbers in each game and adjusting for park.)

There were only a handful of six-day stretches in 2018 that had drag numbers below what we're seeing now, and most were in late June and early July. All of this means that 2019's data so far is quite a bit different than what we saw through most of last year.

118 - The Baseball Is Juiced (Again)

These drag coefficients factor out the effects of temperature and air density, so they aren't a product of April cold. However, the numbers could be deceptive if the radars used to track pitches have changed from year to year. I consulted with some experts within baseball who were not aware of any specific modifications to the radar this year that could produce this pattern, but it's an important caveat of which to be aware.

On the one hand, it's only been six days, and we don't quite have the statistical basis to say that these drag coefficients are unprecedented compared to 2018. On the other hand, we've witnessed about 5,000 fastballs so far this season, so it's not as if our sample size is small. At least so far, the baseball has played like it's much more aerodynamic than it was last year. In fact, the current drag coefficient is really only comparable to 2017, when the baseballs were more aerodynamic than they had been in at least a decade.

It's not just fancy radar tracking indicating that the baseball is flying through the air more easily. The current number of home runs per game (as of this writing) is the highest it's been since the heady days of 2017, the year that teams and players broke dinger-related records everywhere you looked. That's especially remarkable considering that we're in what is typically the coldest part of the regular season, when lower temperatures and higher winds tend to suppress offense and keep balls in the air within the park. Comparing only from April to April, this year's rate of home runs per fly ball is even a little bit higher than it was in 2017.

With that said, the current measurements are no guarantee that 2019 will be another year of record-shattering homer hitting. The trouble with the drag measurements is that they are not consistent from June to August, from week to week, or even sometimes from day to day. Whether because of natural manufacturing variation or differences in the underlying supplies of cowhide and thread that go into the baseballs, drag has a tendency to fluctuate up and down over the course of a year. So the homers that fly in the first week of April wouldn't necessarily clear the fence a week later.

It's possible that this one-week drop in drag coefficient subsides and the baseball returns to its 2018 levels. On the other hand, it's almost equally probable that the ball becomes even more slippery and flies ever farther. Either way, it's clear that the baseball's air resistance is something to keep an eye on for the remainder of the 2019 season.

—*Robert Arthur is an author of Baseball Prospectus.*

The Moral Hazard of Playing It Safe

Craig Goldstein

This article originally appeared at Baseball Prospectus on August 6, 2019.

A couple days prior to the trade deadline, amidst a sea of tranquility posing as the lead up to the trade deadline, Bob Nightengale took to Twitter. Nightengale, who was probably wearing his pants backwards at the time, tweeted that MLB GMs were coming around on the idea that the unified trade deadline should be moved back from July 31 to August 15, so they could better assess their positions in the standings and whether they should buy or sell. To which I said:

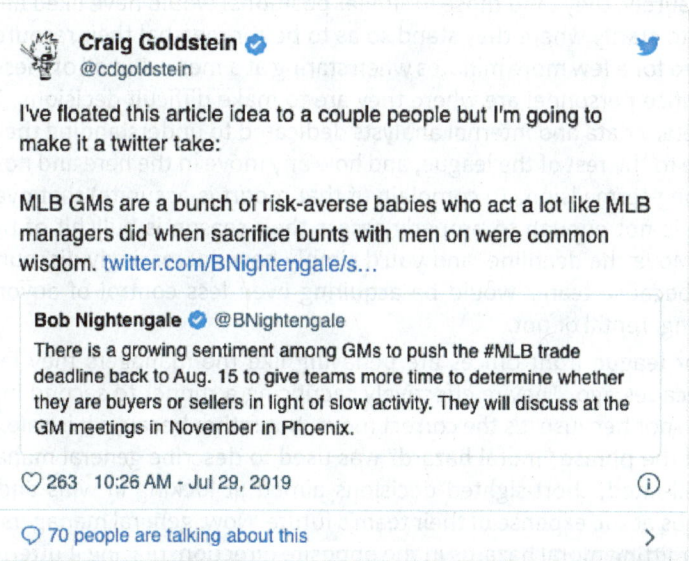

This might strike some as reductive and churlish. And it might be that, but it isn't really wrong, either. Jeff Quinton wrote a great piece discussing the environmental factors that enable front offices to avoid risk without upsetting the apple cart within their own fanbases. I don't believe that it goes far enough, however. His article gives us the proper framework through which to understand why these behaviors have been allowed to seep into front offices throughout the league. Understanding the reasons behind these actions are different from excusing them, though, and GMs should not be let off the hook for their non-competitive approach to the trade deadline (much less the offseason).

⚾ ⚾ ⚾

It's fair to say that fans as a group have rarely, if ever, been pro-player. It is also fair to say that in the time during and following the Moneyball revolution, the pendulum swung from fans who cared intensely about winning in the moment (and thus might be intolerant of a rebuilding approach) to fans who supported building a team that could compete throughout multiple seasons, viewing the playoffs as a crapshoot, with the thought that getting multiple bites at the apple was a better approach than taking a bigger bite in any one season.

There's nothing wrong with that approach, and I still find merit in that argument. However, it seems that the pendulum has swung too far in that direction. Teams are overvaluing some of the individual factors that make themselves long-term contenders rather than attempting to seize a championship when given the opportunity. It's a difficult needle to thread.

And surely, they (and those in similar positions) would have liked another two weeks to clarify where they stand so as to better marshal their resources. We've all asked for a few more minutes when staring at a menu. But all of these GMs and front office personnel are where they are to make difficult decisions. They have proprietary data and internal analysts dedicated to understanding their position relative to the rest of the league, and how any move in the here and now impacts their long-term vision. To complain (if that report is accurate) that over half the season is not enough to properly assess their season is bullshit of the highest order. Move the deadline, and you'd simply have increasingly discounted trade offers because teams would be acquiring even less control of anyone they're acquiring, rental or not.

Major league front offices are behaving like the managers they lampooned two decades ago. They're effectively sacrificing a runner to second in the ninth inning—not because it's the correct move, but rather because it is safe. It used to be that the phrase "moral hazard" was used to describe general managers who made ill-fated, short-sighted decisions aimed at locking in wins and securing their jobs at the expense of their team's future. Now, general managers are guilty of committing moral hazards in the opposite direction, playing it utterly safe and terrified of becoming scapegoats.

In lieu of bold action, they opt to pussyfoot around a current window of contention, choosing instead to play the long game and stack up years of control like they're blocks in a game of Jenga. GMs pass on signing quality players in free agency because the back-end of the deal might look bad, and because they might be able to squeeze out 70 percent of the production from a player who costs a tenth as much. That's a safer investment, too, because it's also hard to prove a negative—it's impossible to prove that Manny Machado would make the Mets a playoff team in 2019-2020, but it's easy to say that the back half of Robinson Cano's contract sucks. Owners, who rule over GM's jobs, are also humans with human brain processes that will always make the so-called albatross contract uglier than the road not taken.

These days, GMs are remembered for the bad deals they make and the surplus value they generate, not the acquisition of expensive, necessary talents that meet their market worth (or fall slightly short while still providing significant on-field value). And front offices know that one or two expensive misfires can cost them their jobs, no matter how many good deals they make.

No front office exemplifies this ethos more than the Toronto Blue Jays. General Manager Ross Atkins had this to say following the Blue Jays underwhelming trade deadline:

This is by no means the first time that an executive will cite years of control to justify their actions, which is often just another way of saying "don't look at what we got, look at how much we got of it." Atkins touts quantity to elide the discussion of quality—either, that of the players acquired, or those given up. Remember: the other teams presumably value years of control, too.

Atkins also had some thoughts to offer regarding free agents back in early 2018:

This ignores, of course, whether the player can create enough value in the front end of a contract to justify the longer term of a deal, and the decline that often occurs in the back end. It also ignores whether the player can fill a need the team requires and put them in a position to compete for and win a championship. But as teams seemingly avoid contention at all, where they might end up having to consider and later justify some of these tough decisions, we still see risk-averse approaches.

Anthony Fenech's article on two trades that recently extended GM Al Avila didn't make got at this issue rather well:

> Passing on those deals was defensible: Both players had yet to break out and trading [Michael] Fulmer—a pitcher who appeared to be a future ace, no matter his injury concerns—would have taken serious gumption, opening Avila up to strong criticism.

Avoiding strong criticism is something each of us can understand as a motivation, but the avoidance of criticism only matters if that criticism is valid. In Fulmer's case, shoving his injury concerns aside affects not only the years that the team controls him (he is currently missing a full season due to Tommy John surgery) but also the quality of those seasons, as his knee and elbow injuries combined to dampen his effectiveness even when healthy enough to pitch. But it was easy to present the then-current image of Fulmer as a top of the rotation pitcher who the team had under its domain for the next five seasons as something to build around. The status quo isn't nearly as often second-guessed as a decision that disrupts it.

⚾ ⚾ ⚾

MLB GMs are risk-averse to a fault. They are ivy-educated and consulting firm-approved, and yet they can't seem to avoid leaving wins on the table in their all-consuming lust for a non-existent $/WAR championship. They are supposed to zig when everyone else zags, and not merely pay lip service to the idea of zigging through a calculated PR plan built on convincing the fan base their approach is novel when it actually apes most of their competitors. Instead they've become far more concerned with making safe, accepted-by-the-new-common-wisdom decisions, such that our prior understanding of what a moral hazard is has become inverted.

I can't blame them entirely, and not only because of the reasons that Quinton illuminated in his article, but also because of the damage wrought by the introduction of the second wild card (WC2) spot. MLB's desire to have more teams in playoff contention has sparked anti-competitive behavior. Teams know now that they do not need to swing big as they assemble their roster because there is a good chance that a mediocre team can either catch fire and capture a division, or muddle along until they back into the WC2.

Simultaneously, the one-game playoff has neutered the WC1, putting an entire season on the flip of a coin like some sort of baseball-obsessed Anton Chigurh. While the one-game playoff makes sense as a way to increase the value of winning a division, it also means that if a front office doesn't like its chances of overcoming a behemoth like the Dodgers or Astros in the offseason, they have few incentives to chase glory. Similarly, the relative inaction in the NL Central at the trade deadline—despite a wide open division—can be explained by the idea that any high-variance investment could still result in only a wild card (or worse) result, given the mere two months left in the season to make an impact.

⚾ ⚾ ⚾

As stated at the top, we should not confuse reasons for excuses. The implementation of the second wild card is just one of many environmental factors that influence how each front office operates. I am convinced that it is one of the larger factors, but I am also convinced that organizations need to shed the yoke of "efficiency at all costs" so that they can instead pursue competition, as the spirit of the game intends. Until they do, we're all deadline losers. ■

—*Craig Goldstein is an author of Baseball Prospectus.*

Index of Names

Alexander, Scott 45	Kendall, Jeren 96
Amaya, Jacob 96, 107	Kershaw, Clayton 61
Baez, Pedro 97	Kolarek, Adam 63
Barnes, Austin 96	Lux, Gavin 85, 99
Beaty, Matt 20	Martin, Russell 96
Bellinger, Cody 22	May, Dustin 65, 100
Betts, Mookie 25	McKinstry, Zach 96
Buehler, Walker 47	Muncy, Max 31
Busch, Michael 81, 106	Negron, Kristopher 96
Carrillo, Gerardo 91, 105	Nelson, Jimmy 67
Cartaya, Diego 82, 104	Pages, Andy 96, 111
Chargois, JT 97	Pederson, Joc 33
De Geus, Brett 97, 110	Peters, DJ 86, 107
Downs, Jeter 104	Pollock, A.J. 35
Estevez, Omar 96, 108	Price, David 69
Ferguson, Caleb 49	Quackenbush, Kevin 97
Floro, Dylan 51	Ramos, Edubray 97
Freese, David 27	Rios, Edwin 89, 111
Gonsolin, Tony 53, 103	Rodriguez, Luis 87
Gonzalez, Victor 97	Ruiz, Keibert 88, 102
Graterol, Brusdar 55	Sadler, Casey 97
Gray, Josiah 92, 101	Santana, Cristian 96, 110
Grove, Michael 93, 109	Santana, Dennis 94, 109
Gyorko, Jedd 96	Sborz, Josh 71
Hernández, Enrique 29	Seager, Corey 37
Hoese, Kody 83, 105	Smith, Will 39
Jansen, Kenley 57	Stripling, Ross 73
Jimenez, Melvin 97	Taylor, Chris 41
Joe, Connor 84	Treinen, Blake 75
Kasowski, Marshall 97	Turner, Justin 43
Kelly, Joe 59	Uceta, Edwin 97

Los Angeles Dodgers 2020

Urías, Julio 77
Vargas, Miguel 90, 102
White, Mitchell 95, 108
White, Tyler 96
Wong, Connor 108
Wood, Alex 79